If NIETZSCHE
Were a
NARWHAL

If NIETZSCHE *Were a* NARWHAL

What ANIMAL INTELLIGENCE *Reveals About* HUMAN STUPIDITY

JUSTIN GREGG

Little, Brown and Company
New York   Boston   London

Little, Brown and Company
Hachette Book Group
1290 Avenue of the Americas, New York, NY 10104
littlebrown.com

First Edition: August 2022

Little, Brown and Company is a division of Hachette Book Group, Inc. The Little, Brown name and logo are trademarks of Hachette Book Group, Inc.

The publisher is not responsible for websites (or their content) that are not owned by the publisher.

The Hachette Speakers Bureau provides a wide range of authors for speaking events. To find out more, go to hachettespeakersbureau.com or call (866) 376-6591.

ISBN 978-0-316-38806-1

A Library of Congress Control Number is available at the Library of Congress.

Printing 1, 2022

LSC-C

Printed in the United States of America

I dedicate this book to Ranke de Vries: my life-partner, spouse, and favorite co-conspirator.

Contents

"Mere animals couldn't possibly manage to act like this. You need to be a human being to be really stupid."
Terry Pratchett, *Pyramids* (Discworld, #7)

If NIETZSCHE
Were a
NARWHAL

Introduction

Friedrich Wilhelm Nietzsche (1844–1900) had a magnificent mustache and a peculiar relationship with animals. On the one hand, he pitied animals because, as he wrote in *Untimely Meditations,* they "cling to life, blindly and madly, with no other aim...with all the perverted desire of the fool."[1] Animals, he believed, stumble through life unaware of what they are doing or why they are doing it. What's worse, he believed that they lack the intelligence to experience pleasure or suffering as deeply as us humans.[2] For an existential philosopher like Nietzsche, that was a real bummer; finding meaning in suffering was Nietzsche's whole shtick. But he also envied their lack of angst, writing:

> Consider the cattle, grazing as they pass you by: they do not know what is meant by yesterday or today, they leap about, eat, rest, digest, leap about again, and so from morn till night and from day to day, fettered to

the moment and its pleasure or displeasure, and thus neither melancholy nor bored. This is a hard sight for man to see; for, though he thinks himself better than the animals because he is human, he cannot help envying them their happiness.[3]

Nietzsche both wished he was as stupid as a cow so he wouldn't have to contemplate existence, and pitied cows for being so stupid that they couldn't contemplate existence. That's the kind of cognitive dissonance that generates big ideas. Nietzsche's contributions to philosophy included challenging the nature of truth and morality, famously declaring God to be dead, and grappling with the problem of meaninglessness and nihilism. But this body of work came at a terrible price. In his personal life, he was a hot mess, the quintessential example of how too much profundity can literally break your brain.

As a child, Nietzsche had debilitating headaches that left him incapacitated for days on end.[4] At the height of his academic output, he experienced persistent depression, hallucinations, and thoughts of suicide. By 1883, at age thirty-nine, he declared himself "mad" — the same year his most famous book, *Also sprach Zarathustra*, was published. His mental state continued to decline even as his philosophical output skyrocketed. In 1888, Nietzsche rented a small apartment in the middle of Turin from his friend Davide Fino. Despite being in the throes of a mental health crisis, he wrote three books that year.[5] One night, Fino looked through Nietzsche's keyhole to find the man "shouting, jumping, and dancing around the room, stark naked, in what seems to have been a one-man re-creation of a Dionysian orgy."[6] He would stay awake all night pounding out discordant songs on his piano with his elbows while screaming misremembered lyrics to Wagner operas. He was a creative genius, but clearly not a well man. And also a terrible neighbor.

Given his preoccupation with animal nature, it is perhaps fitting that it was an encounter with a horse that caused Nietzsche to suffer a final mental breakdown from which he never recovered. On January 3, 1889, Nietzsche was walking through the Piazza Carlo Alberto in Turin when he saw a coachman whipping his horse. Overcome, Nietzsche burst into tears, threw his arms around the animal's neck, and collapsed in the street. Fino, who was working at a nearby newspaper kiosk, found him there and guided him back to his apartment.[7] The poor philosopher remained in a catatonic state for a few days before being whisked off to a mental asylum in Basel, Switzerland. He never again regained his mental faculties.

The Turin horse, it seems, had been the final blow to Nietzsche's fragile mental state.[8]

There has been much speculation as to the causes of Nietzsche's mental illness, which blossomed into full-blown dementia before his death. It could have been a chronic syphilitic infection, which can eat away at the brain. Or a vascular disease (CADASIL) that causes diverse neurological symptoms as brain tissue slowly atrophies and dies.[9] Whatever the medical cause, there is no doubt that Nietzsche's psychiatric problems were compounded by his intellectual genius, which spurred him to seek meaning, beauty, and truth in his suffering at the expense of his sanity.

Was Nietzsche too smart for his own good? If we look at intelligence from an evolutionary perspective, there's every reason to believe that complex thought, in all its forms throughout the animal kingdom, is often a liability. If there's one lesson we can learn from the tortured life of Friedrich Wilhelm Nietzsche, it's that thinking too hard about things isn't necessarily doing anyone any favors.

What if Nietzsche had been a simpler animal incapable of thinking so deeply about the nature of existence, like the Turin horse or one of those cows he pitied/envied so much? Or even a narwhal, one of my favorite marine mammals? The absurdity of a narwhal experiencing an existential crisis is the key to understanding everything that is wrong about human thinking, and everything that is right about animal thinking. For narwhals to suffer a Nietzsche-like psychotic break, they would need to have a sophisticated level of awareness of their own existence. They'd need to know that they were mortal — destined to die one day in the not-so-distant future. But the evidence that narwhals or any animals other than humans have the intellectual muscle to conceptualize their own mortality is, as we'll see in this book, thin on the ground. And that, it turns out, is a good thing.

What is intelligence?

There's a puzzling gulf between the way humans understand and experience the world, and the way all other animals do. There's never really been any doubt that there's something happening in our skulls that isn't happening in the skulls of narwhals. We can send robots to Mars. Narwhals can't. We can write symphonies. Narwhals can't. We can find meaning in death. Narwhals can't. Whatever our brains are doing that results in these miracles is clearly a result of that thing we call *intelligence*.

Unfortunately, despite our utter confidence in the exceptionalism of human intelligence, nobody really has a clue as to what intelligence is. That's not just a glib statement to say that we don't have a good working definition. I mean that we're not sure if intelligence even exists as a quantifiable concept.

Consider the field of artificial intelligence (AI). This is our attempt to create computer software or robotic systems that are, as the name implies, intelligent. But AI researchers are not on the same page as to how to define this thing that they're so keen on creating. In a recent survey of 567 leading experts working in the field of AI, a slim majority (58.6 percent) agreed that AI researcher Pei Wang's definition of intelligence was probably the best:[10]

> The essence of intelligence is the principle of adapting to the environment while working with insufficient knowledge and resources. Accordingly, an intelligent system should rely on finite processing capacity, work in real time, open to unexpected tasks, and learn from experience. This working definition interprets "intelligence" as a form of "relative rationality."[11]

In other words, 41.4 percent of AI scientists don't think this is what intelligence is at all. In a special issue of the *Journal of Artificial General Intelligence,* dozens more experts were given a chance to comment on Wang's definition. In a completely unsurprising turn of events, the editors concluded that "if the reader was expecting a consensus around defining AI, we are afraid we have to disappoint them."[12] There is, and never will be, any agreement as to what intelligence is for an entire field of science focused exclusively on creating it. Which is a rather ridiculous state of affairs.

Psychologists aren't doing any better, by the way. The history of defining intelligence as a single property of the human mind is messy stuff. The twentieth-century English psychologist Charles Edward Spearman proposed the idea of the General Intelligence factor (i.e., g factor) as a way of explaining why kids who were good at one kind of psychometric test also tended to be good at other types of psychometric tests.[13] It must be a quantifiable property of a human mind, the theory goes, that some people have more of than others. This is the kind of stuff that the SAT or IQ tests reveal. And when you give these kinds of tests to people around the globe, no matter what their cultural background, you do indeed find that some people are just generally better at all aspects of the test than others. But there's no agreement as to if these performance differences are down to a single property of the mind — the g factor — that is generating thinking, or if the g factor is just the shorthand we use to describe the collective performance of a huge subset of cognitive capacities churning away in the brain. Are each of these cognitive capacities working independently and just happen to be tightly correlated, or is there a kind of magical intelligence dust that gets sprinkled across all the cognitive systems, causing everything to work better? Nobody knows. At the core of the study of intelligence in the human mind is this utter confusion as to what we're even talking about.

Then we have animals. If you want to highlight the slipperiness of intelligence as a concept, just ask an animal behavior researcher to explain why crows are more intelligent than pigeons. You'll often get an answer from folks like me along the lines of, "Well, you really can't compare the intelligence of different species like this." Which is code for "the question doesn't make sense because nobody knows what the hell intelligence is or how to measure it."

But if you want the final nail in the coffin showing that wrangling intelligence is difficult bordering on ridiculous bordering on impossible, look no further than SETI: the search for extraterrestrial intelligence. This is a movement inspired by an article in *Nature* published in 1959 by Philip Morrison and Giuseppe Cocconi — two scientists from Cornell who suggested that if alien civilizations were trying to communicate, they'd most likely do it through radio waves. This led to a gathering of scientists at Green Bank in West Virginia in November 1960, where the radio astronomer Frank Drake introduced his famous Drake equation, an estimate as to the number of extraterrestrial civilizations in the Milky Way intelligent enough to generate radio waves. The equation itself is full of wildly estimated (i.e., pulled out of thin air) factors, including the average number of planets that could support life, and the percentage of those planets that might go on to evolve intelligent life.

The thing about SETI and the Drake equation is that they don't even bother to provide a definition of what intelligence is. We are all just supposed to know what it is. It's that thing that results in a creature's ability to create radio signals. By that tacit definition, humans were not intelligent until such time as Marconi patented the radio in 1896. And we'll probably stop being intelligent in a century or so when all our communication is handled by optical transmission instead of radio. This silliness is why Philip Morrison always hated the phrase *the search for extraterrestrial intelligence,* stating, "SETI has always made me unhappy because it somehow denigrates the situation. It wasn't the intelligence we could detect; it was the communications we could detect. Yes, they imply intelligence, but that's so evident that it's better to talk about getting signals."[14]

What AI researchers, human psychologists, animal cognition researchers, and SETI scientists have in common is their belief that intelligence is a quantifiable phenomenon without an agreed-upon method for quantifying it. We all just know it when we see it. Alien radio waves? Yep, that's intelligence. Crows using a stick to fish ants out of a log? Yeah, that's intelligence. Lieutenant Commander Data composing a poem for his beloved pet cat? Yes, that's intelligence for sure. This "I know it when I see it" approach to intelligence is the same method that US Supreme Court Justice Potter Stewart famously used to identify when something was pornographic.[15] We all know what intelligence is just like we know what porn is. Spending too much time trying to define either is bound to make people uncomfortable, so most people don't bother.

What good is intelligence?

At the heart of this discussion of intelligence is an unshakable belief that intelligence, however we define it and whatever the heck it actually is, is a good thing. A magic ingredient that you can sprinkle onto a boring old monkey, or a robot, or an alien and create something better. But should we be so confident as to the added value of intelligence? If Nietzsche's mind had been more narwhal-like — had he not been intelligent enough to ruminate on his impending death — his madness might have been less potent if not entirely absent. That would have not just been better for him, but also for the rest of us. If Nietzsche had been born a narwhal, the world might never have had to endure the horrors of the Second World War or the Holocaust — events that, through no fault of his own, Nietzsche helped create.

After his mental breakdown, Nietzsche spent a year at the psychiatric asylum in Jena, Germany, before returning to his childhood home in Naumburg under the care of his mother, Franziska. He remained in a semi-catatonic state and needed round-the-clock nursing. When she died after seven years of doting on her son, Nietzsche's sister, Elisabeth, arrived to look after him. Elisabeth had always longed for her brother's approval, but Nietzsche had spent a lifetime dismissing her. When they were children, he nicknamed her *llama*, apparently due to the fact that llamas are such "stupid" and stubborn animals that, when maltreated, refuse to eat and will "lie down in the dust to die."[16]

Unfortunately for Nietzsche (and the rest of us), Elisabeth was a far-right German nationalist. She helped establish the town of Nueva Germania in Paraguay with her husband, Bernhard Förster, in 1887. It was intended to be a shining example of a community based on the supremacy of the Aryan race — a new Fatherland. Förster was a vocal anti-Semite who once wrote that Jews were "a parasite on the German body."[17] Nueva Germania, however, quickly failed; the early Aryan settlers died of starvation, malaria, and sand flea infections.[18] Sand fleas, it turns out, are a non-metaphorical parasite that can live happily on the anti-Semitic body.

Humiliated by the town's failure, Bernhard took his life, and Elisabeth returned to Germany where she ended up looking after her now helpless brother. Nietzsche was no anti-Semite and wrote disparagingly of both anti-Semitism and fascism.[19] But Nietzsche was in no state to argue; by the time she arrived to care for him, he was partially paralyzed and unable to speak. After his death in August 1900, Elisabeth took full control of his estate, and was able to retcon his philosophical writings to fit her white-supremacist ideology.

In a bid to make herself popular with the rising fascist movement in Germany, she combed through Nietzsche's old notebooks and published a posthumous book titled *The Will to Power*,[20] which she pimped out to her fascist friends as a philosophical justification for their belligerent ideologies involving the subjugation (and eradication) of the "weaker races." Despite needing a tutor in the form of the famous Austrian philosopher Rudolf Steiner to help her understand her brother's ideas, and despite Steiner stating that "her thinking is void of even the least logical consistency,"[21] Elisabeth had great success in portraying her brother as the intellectual forefather of the National

Socialist movement. In the early 1930s, everyone who was anyone in the Nazi Party had made a pilgrimage to the Nietzsche Archive in Weimar, which Elisabeth had established to promote her brother's writings — some of which she forged.[22] By the time Elisabeth died in 1935, she was so popular with the Nazi regime that even Adolf Hitler attended her funeral.

By all accounts, Nietzsche's philosophical ideas were integral to the formation and success of the Nazi Party and helped to justify the Holocaust. This even though Nietzsche despised anti-Semitism and would probably have hated Nazis,[23] advising that people should "eject the anti-Semitic ranters from the country."[24] Having served as a medic in the Franco-Prussian War, Nietzsche had seen his fair share of brutality, and it affected him deeply. He was no fan of violence. He certainly rejected the kind of state-sponsored violence that jingoistic political movements like the Nazis employed. Even though Nietzsche claimed to "philosophize with a hammer,"[25] he was quite famously a kind, well-mannered, gentle guy.[26] Which checks out. Remember, this is the same guy who suffered a total mental breakdown because he saw someone hurting a horse.

And this highlights the grand drawback to human intelligence. We can, and often do, use our human intellect to divine the secrets of the universe and generate philosophical theories predicated on the fragility and transience of life. But we also can, and often do, harness those secrets to wreak death and destruction, and twist those philosophies to justify our savagery. With an understanding of how the world has been built comes the knowledge to break it. Humans have the capacity to both rationalize genocide and the technological competence to carry it out. Elisabeth Förster-Nietzsche used her brother's philosophical writings — born of a staggering human intellect — to validate a worldview that led to the deaths of six million Jews.[27] In this regard, humans are nothing like narwhals. Narwhals do not build gas chambers.

The grand MacGuffin

Intelligence is not a biological fact. This idea of human intellectual or behavioral exceptionalism has no basis in science. We feel in our guts that intelligence is both real and good. But when we look at all the ways in which nonhuman animals manage to eke out a living on this planet — the jaw-dropping solutions they've come up with for solving ecological problems — it becomes clear that neither of these gut beliefs holds up to scrutiny. Intelligence is the grand MacGuffin — a concept we've been chasing in the study of human, animal, and robot minds that has distracted us from the reality of the natural world. A reality in which natural selection has never once acted on a biological trait that we can distill into a singular concept known as *intelligence*. A reality in which our intellectual and technology feats — born of a mishmash of cognitive traits shared by many other species — are not quite as important or exceptional as we'd like to believe. A reality in which the Earth is bursting with animal species that have hit on solutions for how to live a good life in ways that put the human species to shame.

This is a book about the problem of intelligence, and whether it's a good or a bad thing. I think most of us believe that intelligence, whatever that word means to you, is inherently good. We've always looked at the world — and the value of the nonhuman animals in that world — through the prism of our own brand of human intelligence. But what if we quiet down that voice shouting about the exceptionalism of our species and instead listen to the stories that other species are telling us? What if we acknowledge that sometimes our so-called human achievements are actually rather shitty solutions, evolutionarily speaking? Doing that turns the whole world upside down. Then supposedly less brainy animals — like cows, horses, and narwhals — seem like geniuses. The animal kingdom suddenly explodes with beautiful, simple minds that have found elegant solutions to the problem of survival.

What good is human intelligence? That is a question that bothered Nietzsche just as it bothers me. Let's see if we can answer it together.

Chapter 1

The *Why* Specialists

A story of hats, bets, and chicken butts

> Gradually, man has become a fantastic animal that
> has to fulfill one more condition of existence than
> any other animal: man has to believe, to know, from
> time to time, why he exists.
>
> — Nietzsche[1]

It took Mike McCaskill twenty years to beat the stock
market. But when he did, boy, did he succeed.

Mike started small, trading penny stocks as a hobby
while working at his parents' furniture store.[2] When the
store closed in 2007, he decided to turn to his hobby full-
time. He sold his car for $10,000, and then stuck that
cash into his trading account. Over the next two years, a
volatile market and the subprime mortgage crisis saw
the S&P 500 lose half its value, which only served to

excite a day trader like Mike. He reveled in the chance to unravel the mystery of where the market was going. He predicted that stocks would spike not long after the election of President Obama, so he took the hundreds of thousands he had made in penny stocks and dumped it into the regular stock market.

But he was wrong.

As Obama was sworn in on January 20, 2009, Mike watched as the Dow Jones continued to plummet, eventually hitting its lowest point during the financial crisis on March 5 at 6,594.44 points. That was a 50 percent drop from the all-time high in October 2007 of 14,164.43, and was just 3 percent shy of the record-breaking crash that sparked the Great Depression in 1929. It looked bad for Mike. His trading account was completely wiped out.

But Mike regrouped, scraping together a few hundred dollars that he put back into his account, though this time he would alter his portfolio strategy so it would pay out if the market should *lose* money. In other words, he would short stocks; a highly risky strategy where he'd borrow shares in a stock and then sell them with a promise to buy them back later and return them to the lender. If the stock price dropped, he'd make money on the resale, but if the stock price went up, he'd be forced to buy the shares back and take a huge loss. This is the trick that investors like Michael Burry and Mark Baum in *The Big Short* used to bet against the housing market in 2007. At the time, the housing market was considered one of the safest bets in

American finance, so betting that it would lose value was both risky and seemingly foolish. Of course, as we now know, their prediction turned out to be right, and they made a killing. For Mike, however, his prediction turned out to be wrong. The $700 billion that the US government had pumped into the economy through the Troubled Asset Relief Program started to work. As of early April, the market rebounded. And Mike, who bet on market collapse, lost everything. Again.

Frustrated, Mike quit trading full-time and spent the next ten years working at King Louie's Sports Complex in Louisville, Kentucky, eventually becoming the director of volleyball and golf programming. He still dabbled in stocks, betting on long-shot stocks that could potentially make him a millionaire. That's when he stumbled across GameStop.

It was the summer of 2020, and the company was struggling: a brick-and-mortar video-game seller trying to keep afloat in a market dominated by a digital retail environment. Hardly anyone goes to the mall anymore to sift through products at stores like GameStop. They just order straight from Amazon, or download games directly to their PlayStations. Michael Pachter, a video game and digital media and electronics analyst with Wedbush Securities, described GameStop as a melting ice cube. "For sure it's going to go away eventually," he told *Business Insider* in January 2020, estimating that the company would be finished within a decade.[3] Andrew Left, a high-profile investor with Citron Research who specialized in short-selling, pinpointed GameStop as "a failing mall-based retailer" that was "drowning,"[4] which is why he and many other investors began shorting the stock in huge quantities. Like Mike in 2009 and the small group of people who bet against the housing market in 2007, these professionals decided to cash in on GameStop's imminent collapse. On paper, at least, this seemed reasonable.

But Mike didn't think GameStop was destined for bankruptcy. Quite the opposite. He was not only sure that GameStop was a viable company, but that all these short positions held by these hedge fund managers meant that its stock could go through the roof in what's called a *short squeeze*. If the stock price started to go up, investors with short positions would try to offload their stocks quickly to cut their losses. This mass selling would cause the stock to rise even faster, creating a squeeze, and making anyone smart enough to have bought stock when it was worth next to nothing a crap ton of money.

Mike's gut told him that a short squeeze was on the horizon. He began buying stock options, which meant he would buy the stock once it hit a certain price. But the stock didn't move much at first, his options expired, and Mike continued to zero out his account repeatedly. Then, in late 2020, Mike hit it big on another stock pick — Bionano Genomics — giving him a fresh cash injection, which he dumped into GameStop. Soon after, in January 2021, the squeeze started. A series of improbable and confusing events led to a rapid rise in the value of GameStop in the market, including the millions of people following Reddit's wallstreetbets subreddit: They had identified the company as having an inordinate number of short positions, which sparked a coordinated effort to buy the stock in droves. As you can imagine, the move screwed over investors like Andrew Left who were, in the eyes of the redditors, cynically betting on the demise of a vulnerable company. It worked. GameStop rather famously increased in value by a ludicrous amount — having gone from around $4 a share when Mike started buying it to a high of $347.51 by January 27. Mike cashed out.

He made $25 million.

What are we to make of this? The lesson here is not that it takes serious smarts and years of experience studying the stock market to correctly predict why and when stock prices will rise and fall. There was no way that Mike could have known that the market vigilantes from wallstreetbets were either planning on or capable of creating such a historic and artificial short squeeze on GameStop. There was nothing about Mike's gut that was magically more prescient. In fact, as we've seen, he was often more wrong than right when it came to betting on the stock market. With GameStop, he simply got lucky.

Consider a similar story that also involves luck, but with an unexpected protagonist. In 2012, the British Sunday newspaper *The Observer* held a contest between three teams: a group of schoolchildren, three professional investment managers, and a house cat named Orlando.[5] Each team was given £5,000 (about US $7,000) to invest in stocks from the FTSE All-Share index and could switch up their stocks every three months. The team with the most money in their account after a year would win. Orlando "picked" his stocks by dropping a toy mouse onto a grid with numbers corresponding to stocks he could buy. After one year of investing, the kids had lost money, with £4,840 left in their account. The fund managers had £5,176. Orlando beat them all with £5,542.

Unlike the kids or the fund managers, there is no way for a cat to know what was happening. Although some animals can be taught to exchange tokens for rewards and thus attribute arbitrary value to otherwise value-less objects, the abstract concept of "money," let alone "the stock market," exists only in the heads of *Homo sapiens*. Orlando's stock-picking technique was just the researchers' clever way of generating random stock picks to prove a point. That point being that people investing in the stock market might as well be throwing darts at a board. When it comes to picking winning stocks, it's all a big crapshoot.

With Orlando in mind, I was curious to know how Mike McCaskill would characterize his stock-picking prowess. So, in March 2021, I called him up to ask. I told him that I was writing a book about human and animal intelligence. I told him the story of Orlando vs. the fund managers and that it appears as if luck — not knowledge — seems to play a huge role when it comes to the stock market. To my astonishment, Mike McCaskill, who had spent twenty years studying the stock market and had just earned $25 million, said: "I agree. It's a hundred percent all luck."

Now, it's true that Mike had researched GameStop and deduced that it was primed for a squeeze. But Andrew Left was equally as convinced that a squeeze was impossible. Left was wrong. Back in 2020, Michael Pachter was sure GameStop would be gone by the end of the decade, although as of March 2021, he had changed his tune and now proclaims that GameStop is "here to stay."[6] One of those predictions is obviously wrong. The wallstreetbets redditors were sure that GameStop was headed for a short squeeze, which was right. But they were also sure that the squeeze would continue past the $347.51 peak on January 27 and encouraged everyone to hold the stock. That was wrong. GameStop crashed back down to under $50 just a few days after Mike dumped his stock and became a millionaire. Mike got lucky there, too. He agreed with the redditors that the stock was going to keep climbing — maybe climb above $1,000 per share. But, on a whim, he decided that his $25 million profit was good enough and dumped his stock at exactly the right moment. Mike's rags-to-riches story is built on a series of random and fortuitous events.

"Human nature likes order," wrote the economist Burton Malkiel in his seminal book *A Random Walk Down Wall Street*. "People find it hard to accept the notion of randomness." Malkiel popularized the idea that the movement of any individual stock in the market is essentially random — it's impossible to know why a stock is doing what it's doing. People who reliably make money from the market are those who own a diverse portfolio of different kinds of investments (e.g., stocks, bonds, annuities), which spreads out the risk, with the broader principle that the market, over the long haul, will eventually increase in value. Picking individual stocks, or betting on certain trends, is much closer to gambling than science. Which is why we shouldn't be too surprised that a cat is just as likely to make a killing on Wall Street as a day trader.

Mike McCaskill spent his career asking a simple question: Why do stock prices go up? This need to understand *why* is what differentiates Mike (and humans in general) from nonhuman animals. And it's what makes Mike's story so revealing. As soon as human children learn their first words, the *why*s start coming. My daughter once asked me: Why can't the cat talk? A good question. And one I have dedicated my research career to answering. As we grow older, we never stop asking these types of questions. Why haven't we found signs of alien life? Why do people commit murder? Why do we die? Humans are the *why* specialist species. It is one of a handful of cognitive traits that separates our thinking style from other animals.

And yet, this burning desire to understand cause and effect does not always give us a leg up. As Mike's investment story reveals, asking "why" did not give him, the hedge fund managers, or anyone an edge when it came to stock price predictions. Without knowing why stocks move, Orlando the cat's decision-making system produced similar results. And it's not limited to stocks. The world is full of animals making effective, beneficial decisions all the time — and hardly any of it involves contemplating why the world is the way it is. Being human and a *why* specialist has obvious benefits, as we will see in this chapter. But if we look at decision-making across time and species, including our own, I propose we consider a provocative premise: Does asking *why* give us a biological advantage? The answer might seem obvious (yes!), but I don't think it is. In order to help answer this question, consider this: Even though our species can grasp cause and effect on a deep level, we barely used this ability for the first quarter of a million years we walked the Earth. That tells us something rather important, from an evolutionary perspective, about the value of *why*.

The origins of why

Let's imagine that we're in the basket of a hot-air balloon. We're floating gently over the canopy of a lush green forest that coats a cluster of undulating hills overlooking Lake Baringo in western Kenya. Or at least what will one day be known as Kenya. This is a time-traveling hot-air balloon, and we've been transported back to the Middle Pleistocene (now officially renamed the Chibanian Age) exactly 240,000 years ago. It is dusk. The air is heavy and moist, signaling the start of the monsoon season. This area would have been much wetter during the Chibanian, making the area around Lake Baringo one of the lushest and most productive in the region. From our vantage point a few hundred meters above the basin, we can see movement on the ground all around us — two distinct animal groups making their way toward the tree line as the sun sets.

One of the groups is instantly recognizable: chimpanzees. A handful of females with their young in tow, and a group of larger males scouting ahead. With night approaching, they are likely looking to find some trees to build a nest and settle in for the night. The other group is even more familiar. It is a group of modern humans — *Homo sapiens* — similar in number to the chimpanzee group. In fact, similar in almost every regard. There are females with their young and a group of males scouting their way toward the forest where they will set up camp for the evening. Humans and chimpanzees both descended from the same ape ancestor that roamed Africa seven million years ago: *Sahelanthropus tchadensis*. To the untrained eye, this ancient ape from west Africa would've looked like a chimpanzee. Its ancestors would branch off to eventually evolve into modern chimpanzees on one side, and our human relatives on the other, including Australopithecus and *Homo erectus*. You've probably seen this lot in a natural history museum or textbook: that famous lineup of the "origins of man" that has become the basis of countless parodies and memes. After seven million years in Africa, chimpanzees and humans still lived very similar lifestyles in nearly identical conditions to their ancient ape predecessors. We know from the fossil record that humans and chimpanzees lived side by side in this area of the East African Rift 240,000 years ago.[7]

I've guided our time-traveling balloon to this era in this particular location because it's the first appearance of what scientists now consider to be modern humans.[8] They are nearly identical to you or me in every conceivable way — physically and cognitively.[9] And yet, nothing about their lifestyle resembles how we have come to live in the twenty-first century. Like their chimpanzee cousins asleep in the trees, these early humans roamed the shores of the lake, searching for berry patches and animal carcasses. They would likely have been naked, free from jewelry, clothing, or any of the artistic or symbolic adornments that we use today. However, their nakedness reveals some significant differences from chimpanzees: far fewer hair follicles and more exposed skin, designed for sweat to evaporate quickly and keep the body cool as they wandered under the blazing sun. Humans also have longer legs with relatively more muscle in their lower limbs, another adaptation to support our ambulatory (walking) lifestyle.[10] And then of course there are the heads. The front half of the human and chimpanzee head — the face area — is similar enough, with the obvious exception being the chin. Humans have one, but chimpanzees do not. Strangely, no other hominid species throughout history evolved chins before *Homo sapiens* came along. Remarkably, scientists still don't have a clear answer as to why we have chins.[11] But it's the back half of our heads that's truly astonishing. Human heads are round, looking like an overfilled water balloon. That extra cranial space is stuffed with brain tissue — three times the size as our chimpanzee cousins.

There are also some behavioral traits that distinguish the humans. They are holding rudimentary stone tools, which they've used to carve meat off a dead elephant. One of the older female humans is helping a child spin a wood shaft into a notch in an old dry log in order to create a cooking fire, giving her instructions in the unmistakable cadence of human language.[12] The chimpanzees, on the other hand, are mostly silent, with only nut-cracking stones (not sharp blades) in their possession, and certainly no chimpanzee-made fires. They simply don't have the kind of minds that allows them to create these things. To this day, the ability to create both fire and stone blades remains outside of their cognitive capabilities.

Despite some clear differences in cognition that led to breakthroughs like fire and blades, early humans and chimpanzees remained relatively similar for most of the Chibanian. As the period drew to a close some 126,000 years ago, humans began their infamous journey out of Africa, using those long muscular legs to carry themselves to Europe where they would encounter Neanderthals and Denisovans — two hominid species that had evolved in Asia and Europe from a common ancestor that left Africa two million years earlier. Like humans, they had use of fire, spears, and stone tools, and may well have had language abilities to some extent. Humans both mated and competed with these other species until there was nothing left but traces of them in our DNA. Then, around 200,000 years after our initial hot-air balloon trip to Lake Baringo, evidence that our human ancestors were asking some of the important *why* questions that would lead to our impending domination of this planet cropped up for the first time in the form of cave paintings.

Roughly 43,900 years ago, a group of humans living in Sulawesi, Indonesia, walked into a cave on the island's southwest tip and began drawing. Using red pigment, they created a series of hunting scenes — humans chasing wild pigs with ropes and spears. But there was something odd about the humans depicted in the drawings: They had animal heads. These half-human, half-animal figures are called *therianthropes* (from the Greek *theri/θήρ* meaning *beast* and *Anthropos/ἄνθρωπος* meaning *man*). A few thousand years later, a European ancestor carved the Löwenmensch figurine: a limestone therianthrope statue depicting a human with a lion's head found in the Hohlenstein-Stadel cave system near Baden-Württemberg, Germany.

There is really one reason that, forty millennia ago,

our human ancestors would spend time creating art in the form of therianthropes. It symbolized something. When we see therianthropes represented in art from the past few thousand years, it's typically associated with religious symbolism: like Horace (the falcon-headed Egyptian god), Lucifer (often depicted as half-human, half-goat in Christian art), or Ganesh (the elephant-headed Hindu god). The Sulawesian therianthropes are "the world's earliest known evidence for our ability to conceive of the existence of supernatural beings," Dr. Adam Brumm told the *New York Times* after he and his research team discovered the Sulawesian therianthropes in 2017.[13] What is a supernatural being? It is a creature that has abilities and knowledge beyond what humans have. Some experts suggest that these therianthropes might be spirit guides, creatures giving us aid, answers, or advice.[14] This assumes, then, that our ancestors had been asking questions that required supernatural answers. And what could these questions possibly be other than those that underpin all religions: Why does the world exist? Why am I here? And why do I have to die? These ancient therianthropes are the best evidence we have of *why* specialist questions swimming about in our ancestors' heads.

Soon after our ancestors carved the first therianthropes, evidence of novel technologies begin popping up in the archaeological record. Like hats. The first evidence of a human wearing a hat stems from 25,000 years ago in the form of the Venus von Willendorf statue, a limestone carving depicting a female figure wearing a beaded headdress. Although I am sure it's just dumb luck in terms of which ancient artifacts we've dug up, I find it amusing that the evidence of humans conceiving of the supernatural predates evidence that we wore hats. It suggests that our ancestors were more concerned with the problem of why we die than why their heads get wet when it rains.

After the appearance of therianthropes and hats, the human capacity for creating stuff based on our understanding of cause and effect really took off. There's evidence from about 23,000 years ago that a small group of humans living in current-day Israel had figured out how to plant and harvest wild barley and oats in little farm plots.[15] An understanding of what causes seeds to germinate, and how they can be cared for over the course of a growing season was a huge deal. We now had precise control over planning our meals. This is a direct result of our understanding of cause and effect as we developed an understanding of plant behavior. A more rudimentary sense of things like gravity allowed the ancient Romans to build massive aqueducts, transporting water over huge distances and even pumping it uphill. As we stared at a river, we wondered, rather remarkably, why the water was moving, and used the answer to that question to help us build our ancient cities.

These "why" questions underpin our greatest discoveries: Why is that star always in the same place each spring? Astronomy as a field was born. Why do I keep getting diarrhea when I drink milk? This was a question that probably kept Louis Pasteur up at night, leading to the discovery of pasteurization. Why does my hair stand on end when I shuffle barefoot across a rug? We now understand this as a result of a phenomenon known as "electricity." Why are there so many different plant and animal species? Charles Darwin had a good answer to this one (evolution). Anything we've held up as an example of our intellectual exceptionalism — and that differentiates our behavior from that of other species — has the deepest of roots in this one skill. Of all the things that fall under the glittery umbrella of human intelligence, our understanding of cause and effect is the source from which everything else springs.

These are all remarkable feats, and indeed, once this "why specialization" began, our story becomes littered with grand achievements in the sciences, the arts, and everything in between. But then we must ask: Why did it take so long to begin? Why did we spend 200,000 years *not* doing this?

The answer is quite simple. Despite what our gut tells us, being a why specialist is just not that big of a deal. It may feel important, but that feeling is human bias at work. From the point of view of evolution, it's simply not that special at all. Indeed, all animals, including our own for a long time, got by just fine without any need to ask "why." It's time to rethink its relative importance. While it has produced inarguable benefits — like pasteurized milk — it's also the most likely cause of our impending extinction. But before we go down that dark path, let's first get to grips with how being a why specialist differs from the way other animals think about the world.

The bear behind the bush

Last fall, I went walking in the woods under a canopy of yellowing maple leaves together with my friend Andrea and her dog Lucy. Suddenly, the silence of the forest was broken by a deep *whomp* that resonated in the ground beneath our feet. Up ahead on the path, the leaves of an alder bush were rustling. We froze in place, nervous that maybe a bear was lurking near us. I went over to investigate. Instead of a bear, I found a large branch of a long-dead tree, which must have rolled down the hill a few feet before coming to rest against the alder, generating that sound that had startled all three of us.

This scenario is something that animals have been dealing with for millions of years. Natural selection is built on countless iterations of animals hearing a sudden sound, determining what it signifies, and deciding how to react. For apex predators like the Komodo dragon (an enormous Indonesian lizard that has been known to eat people), a random noise in the bush might trigger curiosity as it could be something to eat. For prey species like squirrels, a sudden noise might be the opposite: a potential predator or threat that would send it fleeing in the opposite direction.

There are only two ways an animal can interpret the significance of a sudden noise. The first is to *learn* through *association* that a loud noise emanating from behind a bush often precedes the appearance of a living thing. The second is to *infer* that a noise is *caused* by a living thing. It sounds subtle, but this difference — between learned associations and causal inference — is where non-human animal thinking ends and being a why specialist begins.

Consider the burrowing bettong. This bizarre little marsupial from Western Australia looks like a miniature kangaroo with the face of a mouse, a thick rat tail, and the body of a pudgy squirrel. They were once one of the most populous mammals in Australia, but there are now just 19,000 left.[16] The near extinction of the bettong was due to the introduction of non-native wildlife by European settlers, including the infamously murderous house cat and the red fox. Bettongs, you see, do not have much in the way of a natural fear of cats or foxes. Whereas most bite-sized marsupials would flee, bettongs just stand around nonchalantly. Unsurprisingly, this makes them easy prey. In a recent experiment, researchers compared the behavior of bettongs that had been exposed to catlike predators to those that were seeing a catlike predator for the first time.[17] As you might expect, bettongs that had experiences with catlike predators fled, whereas bettongs that had never encountered a cat saw no reason to scurry. In other words, bettongs needed to learn that cats and foxes pose a threat. As a result, conservationists in the region have been actively teaching bettongs to fear cats and foxes so that they can be released into the wild again as a way to preserve their species from extinction. But it's not easy. Without a natural instinctive fear, each bettong will need to experience the threat firsthand to develop the correct learned association. Self-preservation, in other words, must be taught through experience.

Humans, on the other hand, can bypass this process and learn without necessarily needing firsthand experience. Humans' why specialist thinking offers us two cognitive skills that animals like bettongs lack: imagination and an understanding of causality. Humans are capable of cycling through what primate researchers Elisabetta Visalberghi and Michael Tomasello call an infinite "web of possibilities"[18] in our mind's eye in search of an explanation for what our senses are picking up. The comparative psychologist Thomas Suddendorf describes this imaginative skill as an "open-ended capacity to create nested mental scenarios" in his book *The Gap: The Science of What Separates Us from Other Animals,* which argues that this particular ability is a fundamental difference between the way humans and animals understand the world.[19] In the example I shared earlier, I was capable of imagining any number of animals that I had previously seen while out walking in the woods, like porcupines or skunks, rooting around behind the alders making weird sounds before concluding that it must be a bear based on how loud the sound was. But I can also imagine things that I have never experienced but understand abstractly (for example, if I read about something in a sci-fi novel or fantasy series). In this regard, it can be anything, like the possibility that a meteorite had dropped from the sky and landed behind the bush. This fanciful knowledge is what the philosopher Ruth Garrett Millikan calls *dead facts*.[20] These are facts about the world that an animal would not have any use for in its daily life. Nonhuman animals, according to Millikan, "generally have no interest in facts that don't pertain directly to practical activity. They do not represent or remember dead facts." Animals accumulate living facts relevant to their everyday lives: Bees remember the location of a good dandelion field, dogs remember the path through the woods that leads to their favorite pond, and crows remember which human fed them in a park. But humans accumulate a seemingly endless number of useless (i.e., dead) facts: the distance to the moon (384,400 km), the true identity of Luke Skywalker's father (Darth Vader), or which Paula Abdul video starred Keanu Reeves ("Rush Rush"). Our heads are full of dead facts — both real and imagined. Most of them will never be of any use to us. But they are the lifeblood of our why specialist nature as they help us to imagine an infinite number of solutions to whatever problems we encounter — for good or ill.

The second component of being a why specialist is an understanding of causality. Causality is not just knowing that there is a correlation between two events (e.g., whenever my cat leaves the litter box there is a fresh poop left behind), but an understanding that one event is the reason for the other event (i.e., the cat is making the poop). It allows for a more complete understanding of how things in nature work.

There's a long-standing debate as to whether any other animal is capable of this kind of causal reasoning. There is a famous experiment meant to ferret out the presence of causal inference called the *string-pulling paradigm* that has been given to more than 160 animal species.[21] This is how the experiment works: A piece of food is suspended on a long string from a branch or platform. In order to bring the food close enough to eat, the animal must haul in the string. You or I would do this by grabbing the string with one hand, pulling it closer, and then grabbing the food when it's within reach with our other hand. The principle being that you must secure the string first before reaching for the food. When Bernd Heinrich, the biologist most famous for his writing and work on birds, tried this experiment with ravens, they solved it rather quickly. They would pull a section of string toward them and then step on it with one of their feet before reaching down to grab more. They didn't arrive at this solution through trial and error. They eyed the string thoughtfully for a few seconds and then moved in a deliberate fashion, pulling and stepping until the food arrived. This suggests that they understood the nature of the problem and the causal links involved (i.e., gravity pulls things down, stepping on the string holds it in place). Heinrich concluded that *"seeing into the situation* before executing the behavior appears to be the most-parsimonious explanation to account for the result."[22] In other words, the ravens first thought about the nature of the problem, and then cycled through a number of solutions in their mind's eye, and then executed and achieved the goal. Does this prove that ravens are, to a lesser degree, why specialists like us? Many researchers believe so.

However, one research group performed a variation of the string-pulling experiment on New Caledonian crows (who are usually experts at this task) that challenged this conclusion. Researchers hung the string through a small hole in a board, which made it difficult for the crows to see what was happening as they pulled on the string. When a crow encountered this string problem for the first time, they, like Heinrich's ravens, seemed to understand that they needed to pull on the string to get at the food. But after pulling once on the string and being unable to see the food move closer to them, they stopped pulling. Without the visual feedback of the food moving closer to them they suddenly seemed unable to understand what was happening. The authors concluded that "our findings here raise the possibility that string pulling is based on operant conditioning mediated by a perceptual-motor feedback cycle rather than on 'insight' or causal knowledge of string 'connectivity.' "[23] In other words, the crows had no causal understanding of what was happening — it was all just learned associations (pulling string = food closer) that they couldn't learn because they *couldn't see anything.* Scientists are still debating the results of these 160 string-pulling experiments with animals, with some sure that the animals understand causality, others sure they do not, and many convinced that these experiments aren't designed well enough to give us any insight into the question of causal reasoning in animals in the first place.

Most of the time, it doesn't matter if an animal understands causality; it can still make good (or poor) decisions regardless. If a dog like Lucy hears a sudden sound coming from behind a bush and has learned that random sounds in the woods are often correlated with the presence of predators like bears, she will rightly decide to approach with caution. If I, on the other hand, hear a sound and begin cycling through potential causes (e.g., meteorites, bears, a Komodo dragon that has escaped from the zoo), I will wind up making an identically effective decision (approach with caution). Both Lucy and I can make identical inferences (that is, draw a conclusion about how things are) through completely different cognitive paths: me, through causal inference, and Lucy via good old learned associations.

Here's an experiment you can do on your own dog to show their capacity for inferential reasoning and how thoroughly useful it is for them without the need for causal understanding. Take a dog treat and stick it in your shoe. Now, shake the shoe for a few seconds before letting your dog stick their nose in and grab the treat.

Now, without your dog watching, grab both shoes and stick a treat in just one of them. Have your dog watch as you shake them both, and then hold them each out for your dog to observe. In all likelihood, the dog will find the treat on their first try. Why? Because they heard one shoe make noise (the treat was tossing around inside) and the other didn't. This is called diagnostic inference.[24] It's an advanced kind of learned association where the dog has figured out that a sound goes hand in hand with a treat. It's important to understand, however, that the dog does not comprehend that the treat is the thing *causing* the sound. That's causal inference. But the dog doesn't need it. It still found the treat.

Diagnostic inference, as you can imagine, has its limitations. Here's an example where our abilities with causal inference outshine other animals. Imagine now that I am holding two shoes. One is filled with florps and the other with boopers. I show you a picture of florps (candies that resemble mini marshmallows) and a picture of bloopers (small metal balls). Even though you've never seen florps or bloopers — aside from the photos, you know nothing else about them — the moment I shake the shoes you will know which has the bloopers: it's the shoe making more noise. This is because you understand causal properties of objects on a deep level. Soft objects make less noise than hard objects. Dogs would be incapable of this: They would need examples of the different sounds these objects make before they can generate a learned association.

Clearly, diagnostic inference and basic learned associations can only take an animal so far. Without an understanding of — or interest in — underlying causality, an animal will never ask the kind of why questions that led to the accomplishments that *Homo sapiens* have enjoyed: fire, agriculture, particle accelerators, and so forth. It seems obvious that humans have a serious advantage over other animals when it comes to both basic (e.g., what's causing a sound) and complex (e.g., knowing that viruses cause disease) survival skills thanks to our minds. We are capable of cycling through an infinite web of possibilities and dead facts that help us in our quest for causal understanding. But this brings us back to the original conundrum: If causal understanding is such an obvious advantage over other ways of thinking, why did it take our species 200,000 years before we began using this ability to begin the spread of modern civilization? The answer is that sometimes, being a why specialist leads our species toward unexpected ludicrousness that is so bad for our species (evolutionarily speaking) that it makes you wonder if we'd actually be better off relying solely on learned associations.

Chicken butt solutions

Imagine for a moment that we are back in our time-traveling hot-air balloon, this time visiting Lake Baringo 100,000 years ago. We find our group in a slightly more permanent-looking camp on the shores of the lake. From our vantage point, we are witness to an unfortunate albeit common event. A young boy has recently been bitten on the calf by a puff adder, the deadliest snake in Africa. Without treatment there is a high probability that he will die. Luckily, an adult is rushing over with stalks from a large plant with wide palm leaves called *ensete*, or false banana. When she snaps the stalk in two, a sap emerges, which she quickly wipes onto the bite wound. Though nowhere near as effective as modern antivenom, this plant has analgesic and antiseptic properties (and is still used by locals in modern-day Kenya to treat snakebites).[25] How did this prehistoric human know how to do that? Our ancient knowledge of plant medicine was based on a combination of learned associations and causal inference. There was probably a moment where an ancient Baringo relative cut their arm while out hunting in the bush, and randomly grabbed a few leaves from a false banana to stanch the bleeding. A few days later, they may have noticed that their cut healed faster than normal. They might have asked themselves: Why? This would've led to the conclusion that there was some property in the leaf that helped healing. This knowledge would've been passed on (through language and culture) for thousands of years, leading to a brilliant snakebite cure that saved the little boy's life.

Clearly, causal inference is a powerful tool in our ancestors' why specialist arsenal. But that's not to say that it was wielded correctly all the time. Sometimes our need to look for causal connections creates more problems than it solves. It creates the illusion of causality where there is none.

To see what I mean, let's take one more trip in the balloon. This time let's go to medieval Wales, around the year 1000 CE. We're floating over rolling green hills overlooking the Irish Sea where a group of humans are living in a small village. A century from now, a fortress will be built on this spot by an Anglo-Norman baron, setting off a chain of events that will ultimately lead to the founding of the lovely seaside town of Aberystwyth. But for now, it's just a tiny village of Welsh-speaking locals who've encountered a similar problem to our prehistoric clan above. A young boy — the son of the village's leader — was playing in the tall grass when he was bitten by a European adder. Although less deadly than a puff adder, the bite could still be fatal for a child, especially if left untreated. Luckily, there is a healer in the town.

The boy's mother, who has brought him to the healer's home, cradles his head as the venom causes the wound in his calf to swell. The healer hurries over to the boy, carrying a rooster that he has retrieved from his chicken coop. After plucking a few tail feathers to reveal its skin, he presses the now naked rooster bottom against the boy's bite wound. After holding this position for more than an hour, he declares the boy healed. The boy is then carried back to his home where he dies a few hours later: The rooster had little effect, and the boy suffered cardiac arrest from the adder venom.

This treatment — the rubbing of a rooster's butt against a snakebite wound — was one of the accepted medical solutions to treat snakebites throughout Europe at the time. A medical text from Wales written in the late fourteenth century provides clear guidelines: "For a snakebite, if it is a man [who has been bitten], take a live cockerel and put its bottom onto the bite and leave it there, and that is good. If it is a woman, take a live hen in the same way, and that will get rid of the poison."[26]

The same medieval Welsh manuscript includes other medical remedies, such as a cure for deafness by shoving a mixture of ram urine, eel bile, and ash tree sap into your ear. To get rid of a cancerous tumor, boil up some wine with goat dung and barley flour and rub onto the tumor. Also, there is no need to worry about dying of a spider bite; spiders are only dangerous between September and February, and if you get bitten during that period, just crush up some dead flies and wipe it onto the bite and you'll be fine. This might all sound ludicrous to modern readers, but occasionally — either through dumb luck or an application of causal inference that just happened to be correct — medieval medicine worked. Sometimes better than modern medicine. Scientists recently found a potential treatment for the antibiotic resistant superbug MRSA in *Bald's Leechbook* — a medical text from the ninth century — in the form of a salve made from onions, leeks, garlic, and cow bile.[27]

The history of medicine is causal inference in action: the expert community in a given time and place had focused on why disease happens and how and why people die from wounds — searching not just for correlation, but causation. This led to the development of an elaborate theoretical paradigm — now in the dustbin of history — called *humorism*. If you've never heard of it, don't worry. Hardly anyone alive today thinks about it, and with good reason.

Yet, humorism was the dominant medical paradigm in Europe for close to two thousand years. Western civilization is built on the back of this now defunct, discredited medical system. Any famous figure from Western history before the nineteenth century — Julius Caesar, Joan of Arc, Charlemagne, Eleanor of Aquitaine, Napoleon — would have known about and believed in humorism.

It first arose as a concept around 500 BCE in ancient Greece. The word *humor* is a translation of the Greek word χυμός, which literally means *sap*. It was the Greek physician Hippocrates (of Hippocratic oath fame) who is most associated with the popularization of the idea, which he described as follows:

"The Human body contains blood, phlegm, yellow bile and black bile. These are the things that make up its constitution and cause its pains and health. Health is primarily that state in which these constituent substances are in the correct proportion to each other, both in strength and quantity, and are well mixed. Pain occurs when one of the substances presents either a deficiency or an excess, or is separated in the body and not mixed with others."[28]

The second and early third-century Greek physician Galen and the tenth-century Persian physician and polymath Avicenna are credited with expanding upon these ideas to create the then modern form of humorism in vogue at the time we visited Wales in our time-traveling balloon. Imbalances in the humors described how disease arose. The humors themselves — blood, phlegm, yellow bile, and black bile — were made up of four contraries: hot, cold, wet, and dry. Yellow bile was hot and dry, blood was hot and wet, phlegm was cold and wet, and black bile was cold and dry. These four contraries were responsible for forming everything in the universe, including the four elements: fire, water, air, and earth. Fire, for example, would be hot and dry, whereas water was cold and wet. Knowledge of these opposing forces could be used by a physician to cure any ailment. Someone with a fever would be too hot and too dry, throwing their humors out of whack (i.e., creating an abundance of yellow bile). Treating the fever thus involved exposing the patient to something cold and wet — like lettuce — to restore the balance of the humors.

The explanation for the rooster solution to the snakebite is rooted in humorism, although that Welsh manuscript doesn't get into details. Nonetheless, the thinking was that applying a rooster's behind to a snakebite wound would draw the venom out from the person and transfer it to the rooster. This, of course, would occur because of the magical combination of humor imbalance and the contraries.[29]

Humorism was a beautifully complex medical system built entirely on the back of causal inference. Practitioners were right about the fact that disease and injury involve changes to — and problems with — the many substances in our body that regulate our biology, including blood, bile, etc. They were just wrong about the mechanics of causality. Humorism was eventually replaced by modern medicine in the mid-nineteenth century. Modern medicine is born of the scientific method that incorporates a technique that is fundamental to sniffing out the difference between correlation and causation: the clinical trial.[30] With it, you can take an inference for causality (like rooster butts rubbed on a wound causing venom to leave the body) and subject it to verification. You could, for example, give one hundred snakebite patients a rooster butt cure, one hundred patients a placebo (like rubbing the wound with garlic bread), and one hundred patients no treatment. If you look at the results and find that all three groups had the same cure rate, you now know that rooster butts (and bread) don't really cure snakebite wounds. Working back from there, you can test all the underlying assumptions of humorism until you eventually learn that the inferences concerning how the humors work had been wrong all along.

Of course, the scientific method and clinical trials don't *always* produce accurate results. For the longest time, the scientific method led us to believe that the cause of gastric ulcers was stress — until 1984 when Barry J. Marshall and J. Robin Warren showed that the bacterium

Helicobacter pylori was the root cause. They figured this out after Marshall siphoned off some bacteria from the stomach of a patient with gastritis, added it to a cup of broth, and drank it. He developed gastritis three days later: evidence that the bacterium was the culprit. Unfortunately, it takes time for the scientific method to ferret out real phenomena, which allows our why specialist yearnings to churn out crappy, humorism-style answers in the meantime. And crappy answers to the bigger why questions are more than just an inconvenience; sometimes they are so bad, it makes you wonder if being a why specialist might be the ultimate downfall of our species.

Are *why* specialists special?

We've had our "why specialist" capabilities from the moment our species popped into existence on the shores of Lake Baringo, but throughout most of prehistory, it didn't amount to much. Our population numbers were like chimpanzees for a hundred thousand years. In terms of hominid evolution, it was not until quite recently (i.e., 40,000 years ago) that technological advances like farming — a product of our understanding of why plants grow — allowed us to settle down and, generation after generation, broaden our population at levels that put us on a path for global domination. On the one hand, this proves that being a why specialist has helped our species proliferate to an absurd degree compared to our non—why specialist chimpanzee cousins.

But what does this mean in terms of answering the question of whether our human way of thinking — our intelligence built on a bedrock of why specialism — is in fact special, exceptional, or even good? The fact that chimpanzee and humans lived side by side along the shores of Lake Baringo on equal footing with similar levels of success for a hundred millennia suggests that being a why specialist was not an evolutionary triumph right out of the gate. In fact, from what we know about the success of nonhuman animal species, it's clear that animals can make fantastically useful decisions without the need for asking why things happen, and, in fact, sometimes causal understanding is inferior to the less complicated ways of thinking about the world (like associative learning).

In the final pages of their wide-ranging review of causal inference in animals, cognitive ethologists Christian Schloegl and Julia Fischer concluded that "from an evolutionary perspective, it does not really matter whether the animal reasons, associates, or expresses innate behavior, as long as it gets the job done."[31] Amen. By all accounts, nonhuman animals are getting by just fine in this world without a deep understanding of causation.

For example, humans are by no means the only species that has figured out that plants can be used as medicine; other species have arrived at this same conclusion through associative learning. There is a plant in Africa called bitter leaf — *Vernonia amygdalina* — a member of the daisy family that is used by modern-day humans to relieve symptoms of malaria, as well as upset stomach and intestinal parasites. Chimpanzees have been observed collecting this same plant, stripping it of its leaves and outer bark, and chewing on the bitter pith. It's not a plant they typically eat and probably tastes as gross to a chimpanzee as it does to a human. Scientists determined that chimpanzees only engage in this behavior when they have high levels of intestinal parasites; it does indeed appear to lower their parasite load after ingestion.[32] They had learned to associate the eating of this plant with relief from intestinal cramps. Importantly, these chimpanzees likely do not care about why this works, only that it does. Using only learned association and not causal inference, chimpanzees — and many other species from birds that eat clay for an upset stomach to elephants that eat bark to induce labor — can figure out how to self-medicate.[33]

Here's a question for you to illustrate the power of associative learning. If you suspected you had breast cancer, who would you rather have look at your mammogram? A radiologist with thirty years of experience diagnosing cancer or a pigeon? If you value your life, would it surprise you to hear that I say go with the pigeon? Their ability for associative learning coupled with their visual acuity gives them an edge over radiologists when it comes to spotting cancer. There's actually a study that tested this, and the results are fascinating.

Using a boring old form of associative learning called classical conditioning, researchers trained pigeons to peck at pictures of cancerous breast tissue. After spending a few days learning how to visually differentiate between cancerous vs. noncancerous tissue, the pigeons were given a set of brand-new images of breast tissue to diagnose. They accurately identified cancerous tissue 85 percent of the time. Their accuracy levels jumped to 99 percent when pooling the responses of all four birds. This syndicate of cancer-pecking pigeons was better than the human radiologists who were given the same task.[34]

Like humans, pigeons have the visual acuity and perceptual machinery to be able to notice the difference in detail between cancerous vs. benign tissue, and the cognitive ability to place these two types of tissue into separate conceptual categories. In this kind of task, being a why specialist does not give humans an advantage. All you need is a keen visual system and basic associative learning for a pigeon to outclass a radiologist when it comes to spotting cancerous tissue.

But it's the negative consequences of being a why specialist that really call into question its exceptionalism and general coolness. Consider the potential fallout from the way a human (as opposed to a chimpanzee) would approach the question of causality in the case of using bitter leaf to cure an upset stomach. It's easy to imagine a scenario where the human capacity for asking *why* when it comes to the question of "Why do I feel better when I eat bitter leaf?" could lead us down a dark path. A human might conclude that the plant contained supernatural properties bestowed on it by a benevolent god. The plant might then occupy a sacred place in society and be used in rituals to extract its magical properties. Perhaps the plant would be used in a special ceremony, boiled down into a strong broth that was fed to newborn babies to give them supernatural resilience on their journey through life. As a result, a lot of babies would die from this ritual as the concentrated toxins in the plant killed them.

The history of our species is fraught with these kinds of terrible answers to why questions. The question of why humans from different parts of the world look different (e.g., lighter or darker skin, shorter or taller, different nose and eye shapes) was, according to the nineteenth-century American physician Samuel George Morton, due to polygenism. This is the idea that different populations of modern humans either evolved from separate lineages of early hominids or had been created separately by God. Either way, according to Morton, you could see the differences in these populations (which he lumped into five races) by looking at their skulls, with the skulls of white people being the largest and roundest, therefore containing the most brain material and, obviously, being the smartest. Did I mention that Morton was white? In his infamous book *Crania Americana* he describes the "Caucasian Race" as "distinguished for the facility with which it attains the highest intellectual endowments."[35] We now know that the basic premise of this argument is wrong. There is no relationship between skull size (and thus brain size) and intelligence. There are dozens of examples of people who have had half their brain removed, or hydrocephaly where fluid in their skulls reduces their brain size to a small percentage of a normal human brain, that lead completely normal lives, and even have completely normal IQs. For humans, brain size is completely uncoupled from cognitive capacity. As we'll see in later chapters, there's good reason to believe that brain size can't tell us anything about intelligence in animals, either. It was this kind of racism — scientific racism — that fueled the justification for slavery in the United States and the centuries-long white supremacy that has created untold suffering for millions of people. All of it based on a horrendous (and completely wrong) answer to an otherwise innocent why question.

What's worse, the very future of our species is threatened by unintentionally horrendous answers to why questions. The internal combustion engine is a marvelous piece of technology that allows us to create little explosions that can turn a shaft, which propels wheels or jet turbines or whatnot. It was drawn from an answer to the question of why heat and pressure cause objects to move. Unfortunately, the fuel that we burn to make these little explosions (like wood, coal, gasoline) releases carbon dioxide that rises into the atmosphere, where it absorbs and radiates heat. Because we've been running millions of combustion engines for the past century, we've generated so much extra carbon dioxide in the atmosphere that the Earth is warming quite quickly, which, as climate scientists have been warning for quite some time, is bad. So bad that it is starting to tear at the very fabric of our societies, and, according to the Global Challenges Foundation, has contributed to the one in ten chance that our species will go extinct within a century.[36] So yes, chimpanzees cannot make stone blades or combustion engines because they lack a capacity for asking why questions like humans, but they are also not shooting themselves in the foot, evolutionarily speaking.

Evolution is still deciding what to make of the human capacity for causal reasoning. It remains to be seen how the future of our species will be impacted by our why specialist nature. The solution to the existential threats that we've created for ourselves (like climate change) will be rooted in the very same causal inference cognitive system that created them in the first place. It is an open question whether a solution will arrive in time, or if our why specialist nature has doomed us all.

The bottom line is that you simply don't need to have a why specialist's understanding of causation to be a successful species (and, indeed, it might even make one less successful). Nor do you need an understanding of causation to become a millionaire day trader. Mike McCaskill spent two decades basing his stock-purchasing decisions on his carefully considered understanding of cause and effect within this stock market. But it was really nothing more than the kind of random gamble that Orlando the cat could do. "My father says that I am just gambling," Mike told me. "Had I traded normal I would have been wealthy a long time ago."

You can use your why specialist reasoning to choose the stocks and bonds in your portfolio if you'd like, or you can let your cat pick them for you. The illusion of intellectual superiority over your cat because of your why specialist aptitude is just that: an illusion.

Chapter 2

To Be Honest

The power and pitfalls of lying

What then is truth? A movable host of metaphors, metonymies, and anthropomorphisms: in short, a sum of human relations which have been poetically and rhetorically intensified, transferred, and embellished, and which, after long usage, seem to a people to be fixed, canonical, and binding. Truths are illusions which we have forgotten are illusions.

— Nietzsche[1]

Sally Greenwood first met Russell Oakes in 2004 at his osteopathy clinic in the village of Standish, England, a short drive from her picturesque horse farm near the beaches of Formby. Osteopaths manipulate a patient's joints and muscle to treat injuries and ailments, which is exactly what Oakes did to relieve Greenwood's back pain. During one of their sessions, Oakes revealed something surprising: His osteopathic techniques, which worked on humans, could easily be applied to animals. Intrigued by Oakes's claims, Greenwood invited him to her farm to perform therapy on her horses. It was a huge success. Soon after, Oakes began working for Greenwood as her official equine "back man."

Less than two years after they met, Greenwood learned that Oakes had received a veterinary degree and was registered with the Royal College of Veterinary Surgeons. He had been fast-tracked to receive his degree, he told her, given his previous osteopathy training.[2] She offered to have Oakes run his new veterinary practice out of her farm, which he happily did — establishing Formby Equine Vets in 2006. Greenwood was impressed with his skill, knowledge, and what she referred to as his "natural talent." Soon after the clinic opened, he saved the eyesight of one of her horses and correctly diagnosed a leg issue in one of her expensive dressage horses.[3]

But not everyone was impressed. Seamus Miller, then an equine veterinarian with the Rufford Veterinary Group in nearby Lancashire, was confused by the speed with which Oakes obtained his credentials.[4] As a full-time osteopath, how could he have attended veterinary school at the same time? "He was known to the veterinary community as an osteopath in Standish," Miller told the *Liverpool Echo*. "It seemed incongruous he would suddenly have a veterinary degree." Realistically, such degrees in the UK involve five years of intense, full-time study, which would be impossible to manage alongside a clinical practice. He also had his doubts about Oakes's veterinary expertise after seeing him interact with horses. "We'd been exposed to the work he'd done," he said. "It was not of a standard you'd expect." Miller decided to run his own background check by contacting the Royal College of Veterinary Surgeons, but everything seemed fine. They assured him that Oakes was a member in good standing and that his credentials checked out.[5]

Then, in February 2008, Miller was called out to a farm in Ainsdale to deal with an emergency of Oakes's making. Oakes had been hired by the farm to castrate a four-year-old Welsh pony named Roo.[6,7] Witnesses reported that he had fumbled with the anesthetic (taking more than twenty minutes to mix it), and had a difficult time finding a vein for the injection. When it came time for the surgery, Oakes had sliced into an artery, causing the pony to bleed uncontrollably. That was when Miller was called in to save Roo's life (which he did). Miller reported the incident to the Royal College of Veterinary Surgeons and insisted again that they investigate Oakes. This time, they did.

It turned out that Oakes was not a veterinarian at all. The degree hanging on his wall from Australia's Murdoch University was purchased from an online company that generates fake diplomas. Afterward, local police began an investigation into his activities, and uncovered a long history of fraudulent behavior. At his osteopathy clinic, he had forged lab results to convince an elderly woman that she had heart and kidney problems, and used a fake blood test to diagnose a five-year-old boy with allergies, who he then put on a gluten-free diet. This caused him to lose so much weight that he was hospitalized.[8]

Oakes was arrested, but he had a difficult time understanding what all the fuss was about. He told the police that he believed that the veterinary diploma he'd received online was real.[9] He insisted that everything he had done was motivated by his sincere desire to help relieve suffering in both humans and animals, and that he was innocent of any wrongdoing. In an interview with *Horse & Hound* magazine, one of the lead investigators on the case — Detective Constable John Bolton of the Merseyside Police CID — explained that Oakes "lied in all of the police interviews and showed absolutely no remorse. He honestly seemed to have convinced himself he was innocent."

Russell Oakes had lied so much and so well that he even managed to fool himself. Which is, as far as the human condition goes, unsurprising. You, me, and Oakes are all skilled liars cut from the same cloth. Much like our capacity for causal inference, the human capacity for lying is one of the pillars that has shaped our success. Like all human behavior, lying has roots and analogues in the animal kingdom, but our species has taken it to absurd lengths. As we will see in this chapter, the willingness to both create and believe falsehoods helped put our species on the map. Unfortunately, it might also spell our doom.

The origins of deceit

To understand how *Homo sapiens* evolved the ability to lie, it's important to understand the evolution of communication in the animal kingdom more broadly. How do biologists define communication? Here's one: A method for transmitting a signal containing *true* information to another creature with the goal of altering the behavior of that creature.

Communication has been central to the biological world since life first evolved. Consider the yellow petals of a dandelion. These petals evolved to transmit accurate information to pollinating insects about the presence of nectar and pollen. Insects evolved (in tandem with the flowers) the ability to decode this information. The flower, then, is signaling to the insects that there is food, which alters the behavior of the insects (i.e., gets them to land on the flower). This communication system is beneficial to both parties involved: The insect gets food, and the flower's pollen spreads as the insects fly from flower to flower.

Almost all communication in the animal kingdom works by transmitting useful, accurate information. The strawberry poison frog is a bright red color: a visual signal to other animals that they contain lethal toxins. Now, the frog doesn't intend to convey this information; it was simply born this way and has no idea what its redness means. Frog predators, like snakes, are born with an instinctual knowledge that a red-colored frog is unpalatable. It's not something they need to learn through trial and error. When they see a red frog, they stay away. Being brightly colored (like a red poison frog), having high-contrast stripes (like a skunk), or dazzling blue dots (like the blue-ringed octopus) is called *aposematic signaling:* in Greek, *apo* means *away from* and *sema* means *sign*. As a human, you are also born with an instinctual fear of aposematic signals relevant to our evolutionary history. Humans are wired to be wary of, for example, triangular shapes, like the zigzag pattern on a rattlesnake's skin.[10] This ancient fear might be the root cause of *aichmophobia,* "a morbid fear of sharp or pointed objects (such as scissors or a needle),"[11] which extends not just to obviously dangerous things like snakes, knives, and needles. For those who have a terrible case of *aichmophobia,* even the pointy corner of a dining room table elicits the same kind of fear response as seeing a rattlesnake.

However, not all animal communication is trustworthy. The animal kingdom is filled with species that evolved morphological characteristics that also transmit dubious information. Which leads us to define another term.

Deception: a method for transmitting a signal containing

false information to another creature with the goal of altering the behavior of that other creature.

In biology, a classic example of a deceptive signal is one species pretending to look like an object or another animal. It's a phenomenon called *mimicry*. Stick bugs are the classic example. They are insects whose bodies look exactly like twigs or tree branches. Then there are butterfly fish, which have a big black spot on their flanks (called an eyespot, or ocellus), which creates a visual illusion that their body is the head of a predator. Batesian mimicry is a form of mimicry where a harmless animal evolved to mimic the aposematic signaling of a dangerous animal. Wasp beetles, for example, have black-and-yellow stripes that make them resemble deadly yellowjackets, but are harmless. Drone flies (which do not sting) have stripy coloration that makes them look exactly like a honeybee. The Sanguine poison frog is red like the strawberry poison frog, but it is not poisonous. Batesian mimicry is a cheap (from an evolutionary perspective) defense mechanism to deter potential predators. It doesn't take too many mutations or changes to a drone fly's genetics and morphology to evolve stripes when compared to the many mutations needed to generate an actual venomous stinger. Being a stinging animal is a fantastic defense mechanism, but producing venom takes a lot of energy and cellular resources. By pretending to be a stinging animal without actually wasting energy on maintaining a stinger/

venom, drone flies have found a kind of loophole in the communicative signaling system; an evolutionary short-cut that hijacks what is usually a truthful signal (where there are stripes, there is a stinger) for deception (there are stripes but no stinger).

It's important to understand that the word *deception* does not carry any negative connotations in biology when describing animal communication. We think of deception as something that bad people do for nefarious purposes. But deception in the animal kingdom just means a communicative signal that provides inaccurate information. In most cases, the communicative signal itself is baked into the animal's morphology (like a frog's skin color), leaving the animal completely unaware of the inaccuracy of the information it's conveying. For nonhuman animals, deceptive signals (like mimicry) occur without the intention to deceive, or with any knowledge that the signal itself is deceptive.

Contrast this with the behavior of Russell Oakes. He had conscious control of his deceptive communication, and fully intended to fool Sally Greenwood by misrepresenting who and what he was. He both knew that he was lying, and that Greenwood would believe his lies. To achieve this feat, humans have evolved several cognitive traits that make us skilled deceivers. But our ability to intentionally deceive others has, as always, roots and analogues in the animal kingdom, as we will see in the next section.

Intention is everything

The animal communication we've analyzed thus far can be described as passive or unintentional: It's just a physical property of the animal (like a baboon's giant canine teeth or a bull moose's antlers) that evolved to send a particular message. However, animals can also actively, intentionally communicate. Take a house cat. When a cat wants to convey that she is unhappy, she will swish her tail, and often thump it on the ground. Tail thumping is a signal that cats evolved to convey important information about their emotional states to other cats. It is honest: The behavior accurately correlates with the cat's negative emotional state.

However, a question arises: Is the cat's tail-thumping intentional? If an animal decides to generate a communicative signal with the goal of achieving something, then we can describe it as intentional. What animals are trying to achieve through intentional communication is to change the behavior of another animal. And because they have this goal in mind, they will monitor the situation to see if their communicative signals are having the desired effect. For example, when my cat Oscar thumps his tail as I pet him, it's because he wants me to stop petting him. A tail thump is just one of many signals cats have in their behavioral repertoire that indicates that they're unhappy. If I fail to understand what Oscar intends, he will graduate to another communicative signal that is a bit clearer. Like biting my hand.

Again, he makes the choice (intends) to bite me with the goal of getting me to stop petting him (i.e., changing my behavior). Oscar will cycle through all the communicative signals he has in his repertoire that correlate with his negative emotional state (e.g., tail thumping, biting, yowling, scratching) until his intended goal is achieved.

Oscar's tail-thumping signal is honest in that it is an accurate representation of his emotional state. But sometimes, animals produce intentional communicative signals that are not honest, where it looks as if they are intending to deceive with false information about themselves, their emotional states, or their thoughts. Consider chickens.

In *On the Genealogy of Morality*, Nietzsche wrote that "the unhappy man…is like a hen around which a line has been drawn. He cannot get out of this drawn circle."[12] This cheerless summary of the human condition referred to a behavior in chickens where, if you flip one upside down and draw a line in the dirt in front of them (or a circle around them), they will lie completely still. Why? It has nothing to do with drawing a line. It's because you've flipped the chicken upside down and pinned it to the ground. Scientists call this phenomenon *tonic immobility,* or a form of playing dead.[13] When threatened, possums also play dead, flopping over with their tongue hanging out. It's a widespread behavior seen in snakes, spiders, insects, fish, birds, and frogs. It's effective because most predators will avoid eating a dead (and possibly rotten) animal. By feigning death, a chicken is providing false information about its state of decomposition. It is a form of behavioral deception that the chicken uses to manipulate a potential attacker, stopping the attacker from eating it.

A similar behavior is found in many species of ground nesting birds. Piping plovers, which build their nests in sand dunes, engage in something called a *broken wing display*. When a perceived predator approaches a plover's nest, the mother will take flight and squawk, hoping to draw it toward her and away from the nest. Then she does something remarkable: She flies down to the ground and begins walking awkwardly while dragging her wings behind her. It looks like she has a broken wing. Most predators are quite keen to chase after the "injured" bird, which makes for an easy meal. But it's all a con. Once the threat is far enough away from her nest, she drops the act and flies away to safety.

The broken wing display evolved in plovers to be a deceptive act and is quite the clever ruse. And because she is monitoring the behavior to see if her deception is working, it is an example of intentional deception. But there are even cleverer deceivers out there. A few species engage in a behavior called *tactical deception*, which is the closest thing to human-style lying that you'll find in the animal kingdom. Tactical deception can be defined as "when an individual is able to use an 'honest' act from their normal repertoire in a different context to mislead familiar individuals."[14] The definition comes from the evolutionary psychologists Richard W. Byrne and Andrew Whiten, who introduced the idea in a series of articles describing the deceptive behavior of baboons and other primates. The idea being that an animal takes advantage of a communicative signal that it uses to convey true information most of the time to confuse another animal. True information being a key difference, however. The plover's broken wing display or chicken death-feigning are deceptive by design, which means they don't fit the definition of tactical deception. It's only tactical if the animal has made the decision to use an honest signal deceptively, forcing the receiver to misinterpret what's going on.

Researchers have found examples of tactical deception in primates, dogs, and birds, but my favorite example comes from mourning cuttlefish, which is a species of cephalopods. This class of tentacled mollusks includes octopuses and squid, and are gaining a reputation for having a lot more going on cognitively than you might expect for the close cousins of snails and slugs. Mourning cuttlefish resemble squids and lead surprisingly complex social lives. Living off the east coast of Australia, they congregate in large social groups, which is a sight to behold: Pigment-filled skin cells called *chromatophores*, which function a bit like e-ink in an e-reader, turn each of their bodies into elaborate visual displays. These intricate patterns and shapes are used for both camouflage and communication. Throughout the course of the day, male cuttlefish typically display a distinctive stripy pattern, whereas females display a blotchy spotted pattern.

When it comes to their mating habits, male cuttlefish do not tolerate smaller subordinates of the same sex in the vicinity when they are wooing females. Scientists have observed smaller males engaging in a rare and crafty form of tactical deception to outsmart the dominant males and increase their chances of mating with females without raising suspicion.

When a smaller male is caught wooing a female that a dominant male has his sights on, he will place himself between them. Then he'll do something miraculous. On the side facing the rival male, his coloration changes to resemble the blotchy pattern of a female. On the side facing the female, he keeps his normal coloration pattern intact. The larger male will be fooled into thinking that he is looking at two females, and the smaller one gets to continue courting as planned.[15] What makes this *tactical* deception (and not regular deception) is that the signal itself — the blotchy pattern — is normally an honest signal indicating female-ness. What's even sneakier is that they will only engage in this behavior when in the presence of one male. If there are more males around, they won't bother since different viewing angles will reveal what they're up to. This ability to parse when to use this tactic — if there's one male versus many — is itself remarkable. They're actively monitoring their surroundings and altering their deceptive behavior based on the circumstances. Tactical, intentional deception along these lines is exceedingly rare in the animal kingdom — much rarer than the other forms of deception we've seen in animals. Likely the only chance you might have to encounter tactical deception in animals in your everyday life is when interacting with a dog. Researchers found that dogs will deceive their handlers by enthusiastically leading them to a less desirable food reward if that handler has a reputation for stealing food.[16] They will actively fake out people to increase their chances of getting the food that they really want for themselves.

All the animal communicative strategies I've mentioned in this section — intentional communication, intentional deception, and tactical deception — form the building blocks upon which the human capacity for lying is built. Lying, however, is a different beast altogether. It requires a cognitive skill-set that even the most tactical of deceivers — like cuttlefish — might be missing. One of the key ingredients that sets the human capacity for lying apart from the deceptive behavior of other animals is language.

The difference between human language and animal communication is my favorite subject. I am going to fight the urge to write hundreds of pages about this and instead see if I can distill the explanation into a single, simple sentence. Here goes: Animal communication involves signals that convey information about a small set of subjects, whereas human language can convey information about any subject at all. This pithy explanation avoids a protracted discussion about the structural or functional differences between language and animal communication, and the question of how language evolved from earlier forms of hominid communication. The bottom line is this: There is something different about the human mind that allows for a capacity for limitless subject-discussion.

Nonhuman animal communication is typically limited to letting the world know about an animal's emotional state (like angry), their physical state (like what species they are), their identity (like which dolphin they are, based on their unique whistle), their territory (like dogs marking theirs by peeing on trees), and sometimes — but not often — the presence of external objects of interest in their environment (like prairie dog alarm calls that can convey the location, size, color, and even species of approaching predators). Through the medium of language, on the other hand, humans can literally discuss — and lie about — any subject at all. Humans have minds full of dead facts (as we explored in Chapter 1), and thus have a limitless array of subject matter that we can channel into words.

There have been many attempts over the past half a century to teach animals to use symbolic communication systems. The goal is to test the limits of their cognitive capacity for both passive language comprehension and their ability to actively express their thoughts via language. But despite decades of trying, no animal has ever been able to learn symbol systems that enable them to communicate about anything more than the most basic of topics. Even our most prolific language-learning animals — like Koko the gorilla, Kanzi the bonobo, or Akeakamai the dolphin — ended up with a tiny set of subjects about which they could share their thoughts. Either because they are incapable or uninterested, animals simply don't use symbol systems to generate words and sentences in a boundless, expressive manner like humans do.

This capacity for limitless expression via the medium of language is one key ingredient that allows humans to corner the market on lying. But, as we will see in the next section, there is one even more fundamental skill that, when used in conjunction with language, makes our species the most skilled deceivers on this planet.

Mind manipulators

To understand why humans are such skilled liars, we first need a clear definition of what lying even is.

Lying: a method for intentionally transmitting false information to another creature with the express purpose of making that creature believe something that is not true to manipulate its behavior.

When humans lie, we do so with the intention of altering not just the behavior of the intended receiver, but their beliefs as well. This is a key distinction — and one that makes us unique. Manipulating someone's beliefs requires us to know (or at least guess) that other humans/animals have beliefs in the first place, to have minds filled with thoughts, feelings, desires, intentions, etc. Humans do this with ease, which is why we sometimes default to treating inanimate objects — which we know do not have minds — as if they do have minds. Gary Ross Dahl used this weird bit of human psychology to make millions back in the 1970s. Dahl was the inventor of the Pet Rock — a small stone resting on some straw inside a cardboard box with airholes. By simply calling it a "pet," people began semi-ironically treating the rock as if it were a living entity with feelings, desires, and needs. This kind of behavior is both very weird, and very human.

Humans are constantly making predictions as to why other creatures are doing what they're doing, or what they might do in the future based on our guesses as to what's going through their heads. It's intimately connected to our why specialist, causal inferential nature. For example, I might ask "Why is my cat meowing right now?" The answer? Because he *wants* me to open the front door. My ability to guess what it is that my cat *wants* is called having a *theory of mind* (or sometimes *mind-reading* or *mental state attribution*). We can generate a theory or a model of what we expect is going on inside the minds of other creatures.[17] It allows us to ask why living things do what they do and derive an answer based on our best guess as to the goals, desires, and beliefs running through their heads.

Manipulating beliefs via theory of mind gives you

much more control when trying to alter the behavior of other creatures. Imagine you are being chased by a hyena. If you used theory of mind to guess that the hyena is chasing you because she feels hungry, you might try throwing your ham sandwich at her. She might then eat that instead of you. Most animals wouldn't think of this because they are not thinking about the hyena's motivations. They'd simply run and hide.

Humans are one of only a small handful of animals (if not the *only* animal) on this planet that has theory of mind. Scientists have spent forty years designing experiments to sniff out evidence that nonhuman animals understand something about the beliefs and motivations of others.[18] As I am writing this, the best evidence we have that a nonhuman animal has theory of mind comes from the *false belief* test. This test determines if an animal knows if another animal/person has a belief about how the world is that is factually incorrect. The best evidence for this capacity comes from our fellow great apes. In one famous experiment, a handful of apes (chimpanzees, bonobos, and orangutans) were tested to see if they understood whether a human researcher could be fooled into believing something that was untrue. The apes watched through a window as a dramatic scene unfolded, specifically designed to capture their attention.[19] Behind the window, they could see two giant hay bales, and an experimenter dressed in a gorilla suit. A human actor then entered through a door and was confronted by the "gorilla" (a fight scene that is very compelling to watch if you're a great ape). The gorilla then hid behind one of the hay bales as the human actor watched. The human then went back inside to grab a big stick to whack the gorilla. But while he was gone, the gorilla crawled out of the hay bale and ran away. This set up a scenario where the human did not see that the gorilla had left, and now has a *false belief* that the gorilla was behind the hay bale. If the apes watching this scene had theory of mind, they would be expecting the human to look for the gorilla in the wrong location: behind the hay bale where the human had last seen the gorilla. Using an eye-tracking device, researchers measured to see where the apes behind the window were looking as the human came back out the door carrying the stick. Most of the apes' gaze was directed at the hay bale where the gorilla used to be (and not the direction where the gorilla had fled), presumably because they knew that the human — who had a false belief as to the location of the gorilla — would go there to look. This is strong evidence the great apes had theory of mind; that they were making educated guesses as to what the human carrying the gorilla-whacking stick believed to be true about the situation.

The ability to understand that others can have false beliefs and that this dictates their behavior is rare in the animal kingdom, perhaps restricted to the great apes and maybe some corvids (e.g., ravens, crows, scrub jays).

Understanding that others can hold false beliefs is the key ingredient that explains how humans became such prolific liars. The fact that most animals seem to lack this skill — with perhaps the handful of exceptions above — suggests that humans really are unique when it comes to both predicting and manipulating the minds of others. Most animals make predictions as to what other animals will do not via theory of mind, but through visual cues. For example, when you see a dog bare its teeth, you can predict that it might bite. It's a simple learned association between the teeth-baring communicative signal and the behavior that is most likely to follow (i.e., biting). You don't need to guess that the dog is *angry,* or that the dog *wants* to bite you, or that the dog *believes* that you are a threat. This is called *behavior reading* (as opposed to *mind reading*). All the cases of deception that we have thus far encountered for non-human animals can be understood as an attempt to manipulate the behavior, but not the mind, of the intended target. Try observing the animals in your life and ask yourself if they are interacting with you because they are making guesses as to what you are thinking/believing/feeling, or if they are simply reacting to your outward behavior. It can be difficult to know the difference, which is precisely why, after four decades of experimentation, scientists are still not sure if theory of mind exists in nonhuman animals.

When you observe human behavior, on the other

hand, there is no doubt that humans are using theory of mind as part and parcel of their communicative signaling, which explains why we behave the way we do. Spend a few minutes watching a silent Charlie Chaplin film and you'll see mountains of evidence of theory of mind (and lying) unlike anything observed in non-human animals. Chaplin pointing off in the distance to distract a rival so he can steal his bread, for example. A seemingly simple act of deception, but only possible if Chaplin knows that he can get his rival to *believe* that there is something worth looking at *instead of the bread he holds*. Charlie Chaplin films are built on moment after moment of theory of mind in action, and we, the audience, enjoy them because we can guess what's going through his mind: what he wants, what he believes, and why he's doing what he's doing. And all this without speaking a word.

Include words, however, and the human capacity for lying goes off the charts. It's when theory of mind works in concert with language that expert liars like Russell Oakes finally begin to take shape. Language is the perfect vehicle for deception. In fact, some evolutionary biologists think that language might even have evolved specially to help us deceive.[20] Regardless of how and why it got here, language and theory of mind are used by our species to incessantly deceive one another. As we will see in the next section, our capacity and propensity to lie is fundamental to the human condition. But so, too, is our species' propensity to assume others are telling us the truth. It's this bizarre mismatch that creates enormous societal problems for our species. Problems that, as we will see, could lead to the extinction of our species.

Duped

Leo Koretz was a Chicago attorney with a knack for making huge profits on real estate investment deals.[21] As of 1917, Koretz was managing the Bayano River Syndicate: a trust that owned five million acres in the Panama jungle that was exporting huge amounts of mahogany and millions of barrels of oil annually. Koretz had investors clamoring to buy stock in Bayano, where annual returns were around 60 percent.

A 60 percent return on any investment is absolutely staggering, and many investors both now and back in the 1920s would be skeptical of a fund manager promising this kind of return. Especially since Koretz was operating at a time when Charles Ponzi had just become a household name. Ponzi had swindled investors out of millions of dollars with promises of similarly high returns. The Ponzi scheme is an elegantly simple con: Investors are paid returns on their investments using money that comes in from new investors. It requires a constant stream of new investors or else there's no money to pay the interest that the existing investors are expecting. But unlike Ponzi, who had a reputation for soliciting as many investments from as many people as he could to keep his scheme going, Koretz was known for turning people away. He famously handed back the checks of would-be investors who didn't meet his standards.

The few investors given the opportunity often put in huge sums of money and made a significant profit. They jokingly referred to Koretz as "Our Ponzi," an inside joke trafficking on the absurdity that Koretz could possibly be a swindler. Unlike Ponzi's victims, Koretz's clients were investing in something tangible, like pipelines and oil tankers in Panama. They had seen the blueprints of the pipelines and the contracts to buy the oil tankers. Koretz was, in their minds, the real deal.

Eager to see their assets in person, a group of Bayano investors boarded a steamship to Panama in November 1923. They were keen to escape the cold Chicago winter, and even more keen to see the Panamanian oil fields that had become the source of their newfound wealth. After spending a few days in Panama City in search of the Bayano River Syndicate offices, the investors became suspicious: Nobody they spoke with had ever heard of Bayano or of Leo Koretz. They eventually found a fellow Chicagoan — C. L. Peck — who was with another investment firm that owned land in the area. The investors showed Peck a map that Koretz had provided them of the land Bayano supposedly owned in Panama. "Gentlemen," Peck said, "I am of the opinion that you have been duped." Peck's company owned most of that land. The game was up.

It turned out that the Bayano River Syndicate held no investment properties of any kind. Koretz had lied about everything. Koretz had simply run a Ponzi scheme. But he'd been even better at it than Ponzi himself, having duped his investors out of $30 million to Ponzi's $20 million. Despite all the red flags that his investors had noticed and even joked about, they were still fooled. How can this possibly be?

"We are hardwired to be duped," argues Timothy R. Levine in his book *Duped: Truth-Default Theory and the Social Science of Lying and Deception.* Levine is the distinguished professor and chair of communication studies at the University of Alabama at Birmingham, and has spent his career studying human lying, with his research being funded by the FBI and the NSA. Levine's work argues that, despite our obvious capacity and propensity to lie, the default setting for our species is to accept the things we hear as being true, something Levine calls *truth-default theory* (TDT). "TDT proposes that the content of incoming communication is usually uncritically accepted as true, and most of the time this is a good thing for us," he argues. "The tendency to believe others is an adaptive product of human evolution that enables efficient communication and social coordination."[22]

As a species, humans are both wired for credulity and for telling lies. It's that combination of traits — this bizarre mismatch between the human ability to lie and spot lies — that makes us a danger to ourselves.

Natural-born liars

Humans are unlike other animals when it comes to our capacity for deception. Because we are *why specialists,* we have minds overflowing with ideas — dead facts — about how the world works, which gives us an infinite number of subjects about which we could lie. We are also in possession of a communication medium — language — that allows us to transform these dead facts into words that slither into the minds of other people with ease. What's more, we have the capacity to understand that other people have minds in the first place; minds that hold beliefs about how the world is (i.e., what's true), and thus minds that can be fooled into believing false information. As Levine points out, we're also particularly bad at spotting false information. This sets up a scenario where, as we will see in this section, being a lying bullshit artist in a world filled with gullible victims can be a path to success, as it was for Russell Oakes.

The accepted wisdom is that humans tell, on average, between one and two verbal lies a day.[23] That, however, is an estimated average across the entire population. Six out of ten people claim not to lie at all (which is probably a lie), with most lies being told by a small subset of pathological liars who tell — on average — ten lies a day.[24] We tell fewer lies as we get older, which might have less to do with our maturing sense of morality, and more to do with the cognitive decline that makes it harder to pull off the mental gymnastics needed to keep track of the nonsense we're spouting.[25] We need to think harder and maintain concentration to produce lies, which is why you often see the TV trope of an onscreen detective asking rapid-fire questions of suspects until they inadvertently blurt out the truth because they can't think fast enough.[26] It's the same reason for the phrase *in vino veritas* (in wine, there is truth): It's the idea that drinking alcohol works a bit like a truth serum, where people are more likely to reveal their true feelings (and stop lying) when their higher-order thinking has been compromised.

Once a child is old enough to speak (and as theory of mind makes an appearance), the lies start coming — usually between the ages of two to four.[27] If you ask a child not to peek inside a box after telling them that there's a fun toy inside and then leave the room, nearly any child, regardless of where they're from, will not only look inside the box, but lie about having done so afterward.[28] As countless studies reveal, toddler fibbing is a human universal. Once puberty begins, the lies keep coming. One US study found that 82 percent of teenagers had lied to their parents about friends, alcohol/drugs, parties, money, dating, or sex within the last year.[29] Once a teenager leaves the nest, lying behavior starts getting directed toward romantic partners, with 92 percent of college students admitting to lying to the person they are sleeping with about their sexual history.[30] Lying is common because lying works — since most people default to believing lies, telling lies is a super effective way to get ahead in this world.

An even better way to get ahead is to take lying to the next level: bullshitting. The term *bullshitting* is a legitimate scientific term. It was popularized by the philosopher Harry Frankfurt in his 2005 book, *On Bullshit,* and is used in the scientific literature today to describe communication intended to impress others without concern for evidence or truth.[31] It is not the same thing as lying, which involves knowingly creating false information with the intention of manipulating others' behavior. A bullshitter, on the other hand, does not know and does not care whether what they're saying is accurate. They are more concerned with what Stephen Colbert called *truthiness:* the quality of seeming or being felt to be true, even if not necessarily true.[32]

Bullshitting seems like a negative behavior that would gum up the works of the human social world and sow chaos and confusion. But there is evidence to suggest that bullshitting might be a skill that has been selected for by evolution. A capacity to produce bullshit might be a signal to others that the bullshitter is in fact an intelligent individual. A recent study in the journal *Evolutionary Psychology* found that participants who were the most skilled at making up plausible (but fake) explanations of concepts they didn't understand (a bit like the game *Balderdash*) also scored highest on tests of cognitive ability. So being a better bullshitter is in fact correlated with being smarter. The authors concluded that "the ability to produce satisfying bullshit may serve to assist individuals in navigating social systems, both as an energetically efficient strategy for impressing others and as an honest signal of one's intelligence."[33] In other words, the bullshitter has an extra advantage over a non-bullshitter: They don't waste time worrying about the truth; they can focus all of their energy on being believed instead of being accurate.

The psychologist Klaus Templer wanted to know why it is that toxic, dishonest people (that is, bullshitters) seem to be better at navigating the corporate and political landscape than honest, good-hearted people. One would think that bullshitters would be punished or ostracized by society. But that's the opposite of what seems to happen. Templer asked 110 employees at several large companies how they would rate themselves in terms of their political skills, such as the ability to network with and influence others.[34] The same was asked of these employees' bosses. Templer also gave the employees a personality test to measure their levels of honesty and humility. Perhaps unsurprisingly, those employees who had lower levels of honesty and humility (i.e., those more likely to be shameless liars and bullshit artists) also rated themselves as politically skilled. Others agreed with them. The bosses rated their less honest employees as the most politically skilled. But, importantly, also rated them as more competent than their honest and humble workmates. This creates a scenario where the biggest bullshitters among us are likely to be viewed as the most competent, and thus more likely to receive promotions or be elected to positions of power. Sure, we might not like them, and they might be objectively terrible people, but we respect their political and social acumen. "It's also worth remembering that sometimes these difficult personality types can be useful," Templer wrote in the *Harvard Business Review*.[35] "Good managers figure out how to deploy these kinds of people while limiting the damage they do to other employees."

Lies, liars, and bullshit, it seems, can be good for business. But also good for the nation. What major superpower doesn't have a political arm dedicated to generating and spreading propaganda? The Internet Research Agency (Агентство интернет-исследований) is a company in Russia that has been sowing disinformation online since 2013.[36] It employs more than a thousand people to create fake online content on social media to bolster the interests of Russian businesses and the Russian government. Their preferred method is what political scientists Nancy L. Rosenblum and Russell Muirhead call the *firehose of falsehood* — repeating conflicting information as often as possible through as many different social media accounts as possible to create an impression of discord.[37] The Agency was indicted by the US government for their interference in the 2016 United States presidential election by, according to the indictment, "spread[ing] distrust towards the candidates and the political system in general."[38] Which, if the storming of the US Capitol on January 6, 2021, is any indication, seems to have worked pretty well. Scientists had previously seen how effective the Agency had been at sowing distrust in the US health-care system with a sustained campaign to inflame the anti-vaccination debate that began in 2013.[39] That, too, seems to have worked. A Gallup poll from 2020 found that just 84 percent of Americans feel that it's important to vaccinate their children; a drop from 94 percent back in 2001.[40]

This firehose of falsehood is classic bullshit in action. It is unlikely that the hackers working at the Internet Research Agency are intimately familiar with the ins and outs of vaccine science, or the exact details of the US electoral system. But they don't need to be. Their goal is to spread bullshit online — information meant to confuse the American public. They have no real interest in what is true or accurate, but are instead intent on sowing discord within the United States, and thus making the Russian state look more competent and attractive in comparison.

The evolutionary biologist Carl T. Bergstrom and the information scientist Jevin West teach a course at the University of Washington titled Calling Bullshit, which they turned into a book of the same name. Although the course and book are lighthearted to some extent, with a goal to "provide your crystals-and-homeopathy aunt or casually racist uncle with an accessible and persuasive explanation of why a claim is bullshit,"[41] they do not mince words about the serious threat that the proliferation of bullshit in the internet age poses to human civilization. They write that "adequate bullshit detection is essential for the survival of liberal democracy. Democracy has always relied on a critically thinking electorate, but never has this been more important than in the current age of fake news and international interference in the electoral process via propaganda dissemination over social media."[42]

The country of Finland has been concerned with this bullshit problem for almost a decade. After being bombarded with bogus news stories coming out of Russia, the country rejiggered its education system in 2014 to help teach students how to recognize lies in the media. "The goal is active, responsible citizens and voters," Kari Kivinen told *The Guardian*.[43] Kivinen is the head of the French Finnish school of Helsinki, and the former secretary-general of the European School system. "Thinking critically, factchecking, interpreting and evaluating all the information you receive, wherever it appears, is crucial. We've made it a core part of what we teach, across all subjects."

And it's working. The Media Literacy Index 2019 — which measures how susceptible a country is to fake news — put Finland at the top by a wide margin.[44] The lesson here being that if a person — or a country — wants to get better at spotting bullshit, it takes a concerted and prolonged effort to overcome our default for believing everything we hear. But at least it's possible — even in a world where we are drowning in bullshit.[45]

Is our lying ability a liability or a boon?

Many animals can deceive, like piping plovers or death-feigning chickens. And some animals might engage in tactical deception, like cuttlefish trying to mate surreptitiously. But the deceptive ability of even our closest primate relatives is simply incomparable to our own lying and bullshitting abilities, which are due to our unique abilities for language, theory of mind, and why specialism.

How should we feel about this? To some extent, our capacity for dishonesty requires a convergence of forces that reveals an exceptional mind at work. Being a bullshitter is uniquely ours, and we have seen that being a good liar — or a prolific bullshitter — is correlated with social (and financial) success within our species.

But, in terms of the bigger picture, the human capacity for lying — and bullshitting in particular — has a dark side that might outweigh the good. The spread of dubious, confusing, or false information through the act of state-sponsored lies and bullshit has killed millions of people. From the anti-Jewish Nazi propaganda that proliferated in Nietzsche's time to Russia's Internet Research Agency currently spreading anti-vaxxer messages, lives are lost when bullshit spreads.

We long for a world in which bullshit is minimized, and our societies and decision makers operate from the same base reality about what is real and what is not.

Finland has done a bang-up job of educating its children to both desire and create such a world. Carl Sagan wrote eloquently of his techniques for spotting and eliminating bullshit in the chapter "The Fine Art of Baloney Detection" from his 1995 book, *The Demon-Haunted World*. Social psychologist John Petrocelli recently published an entire book (*The Life-Changing Science of Detecting Bullshit*) on identifying — and counteracting — modern bullshit. The tools for spotting and eliminating bullshit are right there for the taking and have been for quite some time. The current problem is that most people don't seem all that interested in picking up these tools.

The reason for this is simple: Humans have been designed by evolution to be liars. Liars that are, strangely enough, susceptible to lies. This is a problem unique to our species. We are not an exceptional species because we can deceive; as we've seen, other species — from insects to cuttlefish — produce communicative signals that contain false information. And a few of them even intend to deceive others. But our species has weaved the intention to deceive — to lie by manipulating the beliefs of others — into the very fabric of our brand of social cognition. At best, we can educate our children to be sensitive to the proliferation of false information, and to want to reduce the harm it causes. But we cannot remove the human capacity to both produce and believe lies any more than we can remove our capacity for walking upright. It is who we are.

To imagine a world where humans have eliminated bullshit and toxic lying is to enter the world of science fiction. As long as our species has theory of mind, language, and a capacity for why specialism, we are going to be a species that lies and bullshits and castrates ponies under false pretenses. These are the unavoidable consequences of our cognitive gifts. We can minimize the damage through an appeal to scientific thinking, but even those of us immersed in science will remain human, and thus bullshit-prone.

Animals inhabit a world where deception exists only as a small subset of their communication systems. A balance has been struck where honesty is the norm. And when animals do lie, the consequences are more cute than catastrophic, like cuttlefish trysts, hypnotized chickens, or limping plovers. Humans, on the other hand, are wired to both dupe and be duped. This toxic combination is currently sending us down a very dark path. Countries like Finland are actively engaged in a nationwide course correction. Animals, on the other hand, don't need a course correction; natural selection has already generated communicative systems that minimize the presence of bullshit. It's us humans that need to generate new solutions to the self-destructive problems we are creating for ourselves through our capacity for lying coupled with our hardwired propensity to believe. The question is: Can we save us from ourselves before the firehose of falsehoods washes our species from this planet?

Chapter 3

Death Wisdom

The downside of knowing the future

How strange that this sole thing that is certain and common to all exercises almost no influence on men, and that they are the furthest from regarding themselves as the brotherhood of death!

— Nietzsche[1]

Tahlequah was twenty years old when she gave birth to her daughter on July 24, 2018. Although the infant was full term, she died shortly after birth. Under normal circumstances, there would be an expert on hand to determine the cause of death. But these were not normal circumstances.

Immediately after the baby died, Tahlequah did something that would soon take the world by storm. She began carrying her dead child with her everywhere she went. She did this for weeks on end in what witnesses called a *tour of grief*.[2] During this period, she rarely ate. When she slept, members of her family would take turns carrying the infant themselves. "We do know her family is sharing the responsibility…that she's not always the one carrying it, that they seem to take turns," said Jenny Atkinson, who watched the event unfold.[3]

International news outlets traveled to Seattle, Washington, to bear witness to Tahlequah's grief. There was an outpouring of sympathy from all over the world. People wrote poems about her. They posted drawings of her carrying her baby on Twitter. There was an op-ed in the *New York Times* from the author Susan Casey on how best to process the collective pain the public felt at watching this mother grieve.

On August 12, 2018, after seventeen days, Tahlequah finally let her infant go. Her body sank to the bottom of the Pacific Ocean. A few days later, scientists from the Center for Whale Research at Friday Harbor in Washington confirmed that Tahlequah had moved on, hunting salmon off the coast of the San Juan Islands. She was back to her old self.

If it wasn't clear by now, Tahlequah is not a human. She is an orca — popularly known as the killer whale, the largest dolphin species. Jenny Atkinson was also not just a witness, but the director of the Whale Museum in Washington, closely monitoring this unprecedented event. There are many examples of this behavior by dolphins in the peer-reviewed scientific literature: mothers carrying the dead bodies of their infants on their rostrums (beaks), constantly pushing them toward the surface. Dolphins care for sick or ailing family members in this way, supporting them near the surface to help them breathe. However, calf carrying typically only lasts a few hours. Which is what makes Tahlequah's seventeen-day vigil so unique. It was so long that her own health was affected. She was noticeably skinnier after weeks of not eating, focusing instead on pushing her calf through the water. Even scientists trained to dispassionately observe animal behavior were visibly shaken. "I am sobbing," said Deborah Giles, a research scientist for the University of Washington Center for Conservation Biology. "I can't believe she is still carrying her calf around."[4]

Many newspaper reporters described Tahlequah's behavior as an example of *mourning,* as an indisputable example of animal *grief.* These stories were peppered with words like *vigil* and *funeral,* concepts that are bound tightly with an understanding of — and response to — death that we typically think of as the domain of humans, not animals. Some animal behavior experts, however, argued that describing calf carrying as a product of grief is nothing more than anthropomorphizing, attributing humanlike emotions and cognition to animals unjustly. "We dilute a real, powerful and observable human emotion by granting other animals the same emotions so freely without any scientific rigour," argued the zoologist Jules Howard in *The Guardian.*[5]

I don't want to spend this chapter litigating the pitfalls of anthropomorphism, however. Instead, I want to tackle the specific problem of what death means to non-human animals. Because death means *something* to them. It meant something to Tahlequah. But what? This chapter is dedicated to figuring that out. And at the end of this chapter, even if we are sure that humans understand the meaning of death on a deeper level than Tahlequah or other animals — on such a deep level that we should reserve words like *grief* and *mourning* for our species alone — we are still left with a bigger question. Are humans better off than other species because of our understanding of death?

Death wisdom

What do animals know about death? Darwin himself wondered about this, asking in *The Descent of Man,* "Who can say what cows feel, when they surround and stare intently on a dying or dead companion?"[6] Almost 150 years later, the anthropologist Barbara J. King published a book — *How Animals Grieve* — citing countless examples of animals from across the taxonomic spectrum reacting to the death of a social partner or family member in ways similar to Tahlequah. Her examples range from animals we typically associate with intelligence, like dolphins, to animals we don't. "Chickens, like chimpanzees, elephants, and goats, have a capacity for grief," writes King.[7]

The question of what animals know about death (and

thus how they grieve) is part of comparative thanatology — a field of scientific inquiry attempting to understand animals' death-knowledge.[8] Comparative thanatologists want to know how an animal knows whether something is alive or dead, and what death means to them. Ants, for example, know something about death because a dead one will release necromones — chemicals only present when decomposition sets in. When another ant smells necromones on a dead ant, it will carry away the body and dump it out of the nest. But you can trigger this same body-removal response (called *necrophoresis*) by spraying any ant with necromones and watch as other ants carry them kicking and screaming out of the nest. This does not suggest that ants have a particularly sophisticated knowledge of death, and only a very limited way of recognizing it.

But other animals react to death in ways instantly recognizable to us. The carrying of dead infants is not limited to dolphins. It is also commonly observed in most primates. Mothers will carry the body of their infant for days or even weeks at a time. This is often accompanied by behaviors that look, to a human, like grief: social withdrawal, mournful vocalizations, and a "failure to eat or sleep," as Barbara King describes it.[9] But grief, if that is indeed what we are witnessing, is not synonymous with an *understanding* of death.

Dr. Susana Monsó is a philosopher with the University of Veterinary Medicine Vienna whose research focus is the concept of death in animals. She argues that "grief does not necessarily signal a [concept of death] — what it signals is a strong emotional attachment to the dead individual."[10] This sets up a scenario where there are different levels of sophistication when it comes to an animal's understanding of death. The most basic is called a *minimal concept of death,* a kind of death-knowledge that many — if not most — animals have. Monsó argues that for an animal to have a minimal concept of death, it need only be able to recognize two simple attributes: "1) non-functionality (death stops all bodily and mental functions), and 2) irreversibility (death is a permanent state)."[11] An animal is not born knowing these things, but learns about death through exposure.

Monsó explained to me that "for an animal to develop a minimal concept of death, she must first have some expectations regarding how beings in her surroundings typically behave." For example, soon after being born, a young dolphin would quickly learn how living things behave. She would expect other dolphins to move their flukes up and down to swim through the water, chase and eat fish, and make lots of whistling and clicking sounds. But when she first encounters a dead dolphin, she will notice that none of these things are occurring. And if she observes the dead dolphin long enough, she will learn that it's a permanent state. Her mind will then be able to categorize the world into living and no-longer-living things. Monsó argues that a minimal concept of death is "relatively easy to acquire and fairly widespread in nature." It does not require particularly complex cognition. Grief, then, can crop up as a rather straightforward emotional response to the permanent nonfunctionality of a social partner or family member.

It's important to understand, however, that just because a dolphin can recognize death, it does not mean she *understands her own mortality.* Or that all living things must die. These are two additional levels of understanding that nonhuman animals lack. According to Monsó, "a very sophisticated notion of personal mortality also incorporates the notions of inevitability, unpredictability, and causality. They might acquire, through an accumulation of experiences with death, a notion that they *can* die, but probably not that they *will* die. I think that such a notion is probably restricted to humans."

There seems to be consensus among scientists and philosophers that there is a fundamental difference between what animals and humans understand about death, especially the awareness of mortality itself. "Among animals," writes King in *How Animals Grieve,* "we alone fully anticipate the inevitability of death." This is called *mortality salience:* the scientific term for an ability to know that you — and everyone else — will one day die. I prefer the more poetic term *death wisdom.*

When my daughter was eight, we heard her crying in her room not long after we read her a bedtime story and said good night. She was sitting up in bed looking particularly miserable. She explained that she was thinking about death, and that one day she would close her eyes and never open them again. Never see, or think, or feel anything anymore. She was scared, but also described a kind of existential dread that was new to her. I suspect that it's a feeling you, too, recognize: the crush of sadness that overwhelms the mind when contemplating the reality of one's own death. It was not something that my daughter had ever spoken about — or experienced — before that moment. And it was heartbreaking to watch.

A question arises: What are the cognitive capacities that we possess — and that nonhuman animals do not — that give rise to our deep understanding of death?

Time and the curse of the awkward fraction

According to Susana Monsó, the minimal concept of death that animals possess "requires neither an *explicit concept of time* nor much by way of *mental time travel* or *episodic foresight*." These are cognitive ingredients — possibly unique to the human mind — that are required for death wisdom. I will deal with each of these in turn so we can see just what it is that gives our species its deep understanding of death. Let's start first with the *explicit concept of time*.

An explicit concept of time is the understanding that there will be a tomorrow, and a day after, and a day after that. This knowledge can extend to just a few hours into the future, but also days, years, or millennia. It's explicit insofar as this knowledge is something that we can

97

analyze with our conscious minds, and thus understand and think about conceptually. The main benefit of the explicit knowledge that time marches forward is that you can plan for the future.

By contrast, an animal doesn't need any real understanding of what time or "the future" is to nonetheless eke out a perfectly respectable living. A house cat, for example, could simply eat when they are hungry and sleep when they are tired, without any interest in what tomorrow might bring. Nietzsche believed that this gave animals an edge over humans.

"[T]he animal lives unhistorically: for it is contained in the present, like a number without any awkward fraction left over."[12]

Nietzsche was lamenting how animals likely suffer less than humans because they are unburdened by the knowledge of the past, and wholly unaware of what their future holds. Nietzsche believed that animals, like children, "play in blissful blindness between the hedges of the past and future."

This idea — that animals live their lives stuck in the present — is widespread, and a subject of long-standing debate for scientists. Except for a handful of cases that we will learn about in this section, it doesn't appear as if many species have an explicit concept of time by human standards. While animals don't ruminate on the future, time is still meaningful to them. They might not have an explicit understanding of what time means conceptually, but almost all living things have an *implicit* concept of time baked into their DNA.

"The physiological, biochemical, and behavioral lives of all animals are organized around the twenty-four-hour day," says Michael Cardinal-Aucoin, professor of biology at Lakehead University, and a specialist in circadian biology. "Their lives are timed; they anticipate regularly occurring, cyclical events."

As mammals, we're deeply affected by one cyclical event in particular: sunrise. As I am writing these words, the predicted length of this day is twenty-three hours, fifty-nine minutes, and 59.9988876 seconds. The moon drifts farther from and closer to the Earth throughout the course of a day. This means that the moon's gravitational pull on Earth is not constant, which in turn means that the Earth's rotational speed is always in flux. Because of this, an Earth day is rarely exactly twenty-four hours long. On average, the moon drifts about two inches farther away from the Earth each year, which is why the length of an Earth day has been slowly expanding over the millennia. Seventy million years ago, there were only twenty-three and a half hours in a day.[13]

These fluctuations and changes to the length of a day are — in the grand scheme of things — minimal, which has allowed many species to evolve behavioral patterns that are based on the reliability of the rising and setting of the sun. Humans, for example, use natural light to calibrate our internal clocks. Like many mammal species, we sleep when the sun goes down. As the light fades toward the end of the day, our pineal glands produce the hormone melatonin, which serves as a signal to our brain that it's time to sleep.[14] This coincides with a buildup of a chemical called *adenosine*, which accumulates slowly in our brains throughout the course of the day and reaches critical levels soon after the sun goes down, generating that feeling of sleepiness that ultimately obliges us to go to bed. Other species, like nocturnal bats, are active at night, and thus have opposite sleep generation systems: They get sleepy when the sun rises. In both cases, the sun serves as a reliable indicator of the passage of time.

There is a more ancient system for keeping track of time in the cells of all living creatures that doesn't involve light. "There is a molecular mechanism in our cells that marks the passage of time," Cardinal-Aucoin told me. This internal clock system is regulated by *clock genes* in our DNA. Once activated, these genes begin producing proteins — called *PER proteins* — that trickle into the cell during the night. Eventually, enough proteins will be produced that a threshold is reached and the clock genes stop making proteins. The PER proteins then slowly break apart until their numbers are so reduced that the clock genes turn back on and start making proteins again. This process takes almost exactly twenty-four hours — one full rotation of the Earth. This mechanism, called the *transcription-translation feedback loop* (TTFL), is found in the cells of most living things, from plants to bacteria to humans. It helps explain why all living things on the Earth — including animals that live in dark caves or at the bottom of the ocean where light does not penetrate — are nonetheless sensitive to the twenty-four-hour sun cycle. Jeffrey C. Hall, Michael Rosbash, and Michael W. Young were awarded the Nobel Prize in Medicine in 2017 for their discovery of clock genes in the 1980s. Before their discovery, scientists knew that humans (and other animals) had an internal clock that didn't need the sun to calibrate itself, but the discovery of the TTFL gave us the explanation as to how our cells pulled this off.

The ancient, cellular response to the passage of time via the TTFL and the external cues from the sun that tell us where we are in the day/night cycle do not necessarily translate into an explicit awareness of time, however. It's exceedingly unlikely that cats, for example, think about time in the way that humans do. My cat Oscar is, like all domestic cats, crepuscular: most active at dawn and dusk. Like other mammals, his cells use the TTFL to regulate his internal clock, and his brain uses the relative amount of sunlight to induce or suppress his morning/evening activity through the release of hormones. He is sensitive to the passage of time. But this doesn't translate into Oscar knowing what abstract time concepts like "tomorrow" mean, let alone the concept of "next winter." This kind of explicit knowledge requires those other cognitive skills that Susana Monsó mentioned when it comes to the human capacity for death wisdom: mental time travel and episodic foresight.

Picture yourself in a boat on a river

Cast your mind back to last night. Do you remember what you ate for supper? Do you remember if you enjoyed the meal? Do you remember where you were sitting while you ate? Chances are you can recall quite a lot. Maybe you have a strong visual memory of what you ate, as if it were a photograph imprinted in your mind. Or maybe the memory is encoded by language: the names of the dishes and ingredients and so forth. Maybe it's recalled through a sensation, like pleasure or disgust.

Now imagine yourself eating supper tomorrow night. Imagine it's a plate of spaghetti with Bolognese sauce, and you are seated on your best friend's living room floor. You don't have a fork or spoon, so you are eating the spaghetti with your hands. And your friend is singing "My Heart Will Go On," the theme song to the 1997 film *Titanic*. It's an odd scenario, totally unique, and I use it to illustrate just how special our powers of imagination can be. You can envision something that may never happen, but you can envision it all the same.

The ability to both recall the past and think about the future is called *mental time travel*. It is succinctly defined by the psychologists Thomas Suddendorf and Michael Corballis as "the faculty that allows humans to mentally project themselves backward in time to relive, or forward to prelive, events."[15] It's intimately tied to another cognitive capacity called *episodic foresight*, which is the ability to mentally project yourself into the future to simulate imagined events and potential outcomes."[16] We have access to an infinite array of imagined scenarios in which we can be placed at the center. You can ask yourself the question "What might happen if I ate spaghetti with my hands" and imagine the many possible outcomes, including scary ones. For example, in one of those scenarios you might choke to death on undercooked spaghetti.

For an animal to have humanlike death wisdom, they, too, would require a capacity for episodic foresight. But for most species, there is little evidence that they do. Which seems, on the face of it, strange. How do animals plan for the future if they cannot imagine themselves in it?

To help figure this out, let's consider the legendary future-planning skills of the Clark's nutcracker. This little bird is a member of the corvid family (like its cousins the crow and the raven) and was named after William Clark (of Lewis and Clark fame) who discovered it during his infamous expedition over the Rocky Mountains back in the early 1800s. While Clark is given credit for the discovery, he, of course, wasn't the first to see the bird. The Shoshoni, for example, had already been using the name *tookottsi* for the nutcracker for close to a thousand years before Clark arrived on the scene.[17] As such,

I'll use the Shoshoni term over the more common "Clark's nutcracker."

The tookottsi's main food source is the seeds of pine trees, which are plentiful during the fall season, but scarce during winter. So, the tookottsi have mastered the art of hoarding. In the fall, they will pick the seeds out of pine cones and hide (also known as "cache") them all over their home territory — as far as twenty miles away — so they can access them throughout the winter months. They bury a dozen or so at a time just a few inches under the ground, making it difficult for squirrels or other birds to find. Tookottsis can hide close to 100,000 seeds in as many as ten thousand separate caches[18,19] in a given season. And, rather astonishingly, they can remember the location of most of these caches for up to nine months.[20]

It certainly seems as if the tookottsi is future-planning, using episodic foresight to imagine themselves in a wintery landscape where food is scarce, and where storing seeds is the best way to prevent starvation. But this is not the case. A tookottsi born in the spring will go through the seed-caching process even though it has never experienced a seed-scarce winter. It is planning for a future it could not possibly know about or imagine. The mechanism driving food-caching in the tookottsi's mind is rooted in its evolutionary history, an instinct for caching that does not require the animal to imagine itself in future scenarios. Almost all examples of animals planning for the future — bees collecting nectar and making honey for winter, crows building a nest for their eggs — can be attributed to these instinctual drives and not mental time travel.

The German psychologist Doris Bischof-Köhler once famously proposed that only humans have the ability to mentally time travel in such a way that they can imagine and thus plan for a future motivational state that conflicts with a current motivational state.[21] There are, however, a couple of animal species that seem capable of this, and are thus the best examples we have of the capacity for mental time travel in nonhuman animals. As is often the case, the best examples come from our closest relatives: chimpanzees. To properly digest this example, you need to know something important about their behavior. Are you familiar with that movie and television trope about chimpanzees throwing things when they are angry, including their poop? Well, it's true. Here's what the Jane Goodall Institute has to say about poop-flinging:

> In their natural habitat, when chimpanzees become angry, they often stand up, wave their arms, and throw branches or rocks — anything nearby that they can get their hands on. Captive chimpanzees are deprived of the diverse objects they would find in nature, and the most readily available projectile is feces. Since they also tend to get a pretty strong reaction from people when they do throw it, their behaviour is reinforced and likely to be repeated,

which explains the abundance of YouTube videos on this subject.[22]

Now, allow me to introduce you to Santino, whose object-throwing wrath is world famous. Born in 1978, Santino is a male chimpanzee living at the Furuvik zoo in Sweden. He has long had a reputation for throwing stones at the human tourists gathered in the designated viewing area near his enclosure. In 1997, zookeepers noticed that Santino seemed to be hurling an unusually large number of projectiles (mostly rocks, not feces) over the course of a couple of days. When they went into his enclosure to investigate, they found a stockpile of stones and other objects hidden under vegetation along the shores of the moat near the tourist viewing area. There were even pieces of concrete that he had lugged over from the far side of his enclosure. Researchers later discovered that Santino would spend hours before the zoo opened collecting and stashing his stones in preparation.[23,24]

Now, as we saw with the tookottsi, stashing things is not evidence of sophisticated future planning that necessarily involves episodic foresight. What makes Santino's behavior special, however, is that he was preparing his stockpile long before he was overcome with fits of rock-throwing rage. By all accounts, he seemed calm while creating his stockpiles. This suggests that Santino was preparing for a future in which he knew he was going to feel angry (even though he was not feeling angry in that moment). Unlike the tookottsi, Santino seemed to be time traveling in his mind and using those memories to imagine himself in future scenarios. Because Santino appears to have been imagining a future in which he felt differently from the way he was feeling in the moment, he challenges the Bischof-Köhler hypothesis that this is a human-only trait. Mathias Osvath, the lead researcher studying Santino's behavior, stated that "the accumulating weight of data throws grave doubt on the notion that the episodic cognitive system is exclusive to humans."[25]

Another challenge to Bischof-Köhler's hypothesis comes from western scrub jays. Scrub jays are corvids, like crows, ravens, and the tookottsi. Like other corvids, scrub jays cache food. In one famous experiment, jays were kept overnight in one of two cages: one in which they received dog kibble for breakfast, and one in which they received peanuts for breakfast. They never knew which cage they might end up in for the night, and thus couldn't be sure what food they'd be having for breakfast. For the experiment, the jays were allowed to eat as much food as they wanted during the day (and were thus no longer hungry) and were then given access to peanuts and kibble that they could then stash in either (or both) of the overnight compartments. The birds ended up caching most of the kibble in the cage where peanuts were the usual breakfast food, and cached more peanuts in the cage where kibble was the usual breakfast food. In other words, they were planning it so that no matter which compartment they were stuck in for the night, they could wake up to a breakfast consisting of both peanuts *and* kibble.

The key thing to remember is that the jays were not hungry while they were caching food. Instead, they were imagining a scenario where they would be. "The western scrub-jays demonstrate behaviour that shows they are concerned both about guarding against food shortages and maximising the variety of their diets," explained Nicola Clayton, one of the authors of the study.[26] "Jays can spontaneously plan for tomorrow without reference to their current motivational state, thereby challenging the idea that this is a uniquely human ability."[27]

These are the best examples we have of animals possessing and acting on a capacity for episodic foresight. As impressive as they are, there are two important things to note here. First, if animals do have episodic foresight like humans, it doesn't seem to be particularly widespread. Second, these species do not seem to use their mental time traveling abilities to the same extent as humans. They seem to mostly plan for the (near) future as it relates to the acquisition of food. I don't mean to downplay these examples because they rather elegantly (in my opinion) demonstrate that episodic foresight does indeed exist in nonhuman minds. But they also demonstrate the limits of animals' foresight abilities in that, for whatever reason, animals don't seem able to use this skill for anything other than food acquisition (and assaulting zoo visitors).

So what does this tell us about animals' capacity for death wisdom?

This is what we know: Most animals have a minimal concept of death. They know that death means a previously living thing has entered a state of permanent nonfunctionality. We know that natural selection can give animals an ability to plan through instinctual behavior that does not rely on an explicit concept of time, nor any form of mental time travel or episodic foresight. We know that most animal species, like the tookottsi, can prepare for their future just fine without needing episodic foresight. And despite evidence for episodic foresight in some species (e.g., chimpanzees, western scrub jays), there is no scientific evidence that nonhuman animals can think about or plan for an unlimited number of future situations, including their own death. This is in stark contrast to humans. Death wisdom appears to be the domain of our species and likely our species alone. The question then becomes: Is this a good or a bad thing? In terms of natural selection (and our own sanity), is death wisdom a boon, or a curse?

The curse of Kassandra

The field of evolutionary thanatology was first introduced in 2018 as a new academic discipline focusing on how animals (including humans) evolved their understanding of — and behavioral responses to — death.[28] Modern humans, as you well know, do not treat our dead in the same way as any other animal species. We have elaborate cultural rules and rituals. The ancient Egyptians from the Old Kingdom (2686 to 2125 BCE) famously mummified the bodies of the elite members of society, placed their organs (stomach, intestines, liver, and lungs) in canopic jars, and preserved the body in linen bandages. The heart was left untouched, and the brain was removed and discarded. In modern-day South Korea, bodies are cremated and the ashes are compressed into shiny beads that can be worn as jewelry. At some funeral homes in North America, visitors are given a drive-in option, allowing the bereaved to stay in their cars as they roll by their loved one's coffin.

Evolutionary thanatology is dedicated to understanding not just how these human funerary practices evolved culturally, but how our psychological understanding and responses to death evolved over time. Since it can be rather difficult to probe the psychology of species that have been dead for millions of years, a much easier place to start is to look at our closest living relative: chimpanzees. In a series of articles unveiling the field of evolutionary thanatology, the psychologist James Anderson considered what we know (and don't know) about chimpanzees' understanding of death, writing:

> Whether chimpanzees understand that all creatures will die (universality) is less clear, but a reasonable suggestion is that they know that other creatures

can die. This knowledge probably includes a notion of their own vulnerability, if not the inevitability of their own death.[29]

An understanding of the inevitability of one's death is the key difference between human and animal psychology where death is concerned. Humans know our death is inevitable. Chimpanzees might understand this, but, based on the scientific evidence mentioned, probably don't. This means that somewhere during the evolution of *Homo sapiens* from the common ancestor we shared with chimpanzees, we split with our closest ape relatives when it came to our capacity to envision our deaths. Something happened in our ancestors' brains/minds that turned our minimal concept of death into full-blown death wisdom.

Imagine, then, the very moment that a genetic mutation cropped up in a hominid genome that led to a baby being born with, for the first time, the cognitive capacity to learn that its death is unavoidable. This is not just a hypothetical scenario, but a real event that occurred somewhere in the past seven million years. It's unlikely that a single mutation would have caused a death wisdom gene to pop into existence out of nothing, of course. It would've been a natural selection process that transpired over the course of millennia building upon a collection of evolving cognitive skills — like those needed for mental time travel or episodic foresight. But there was undeniably a moment in our species' history where a hominid baby was born with a full capacity for mortality salience to parents that lacked this capacity to the same extent. A moment when death wisdom blossomed in the mind of a child for the first time in the history of life on this planet.

Imagine that poor child, growing up somewhere in Africa. Let's call her Kassandra. During puberty, and after a lifetime of learning about death by witnessing family members and the animals around her die, Kassandra would feel the first pain of death wisdom grip her mind. Like it did for my daughter around the age of eight. If Kassandra were to try to explain the nature of her anxiety to her parents using whatever language capacity her species had at the time, her parents simply wouldn't understand. She would be living in a private hell of existential angst with literally nobody on the planet who could understand what she was going through.

How did this newfound knowledge benefit that young girl? There's every reason to believe that death wisdom bursting into a young mind like that would cause so much trauma that Kassandra would be unable to function normally. At the very least, it's difficult to see how this knowledge would increase her fitness, evolutionarily speaking. Kassandra's parents and siblings were surely already struggling to eke out a living, as was the norm for our prehistoric ancestors. They already lived in fear. What possible benefit could there be to *knowing* she would one day die? This young girl should, by all accounts, have suffered enough psychological trauma to end her genetic line then and there.

But that did not happen. Instead, Kassandra's genetic line became the dominant one. Her success as an individual within her family and tribe led to the spread of death wisdom to the entire species. And from Kassandra's genetic stock sprang *Homo sapiens,* not only the last hominid species standing, but the single most successful mammalian species ever to walk this planet.

How did Kassandra manage this? In the book *Denial: Self-Deception, False Beliefs, and the Origins of the Human Mind,* the physician Ajit Varki explains how a conversation with the late biologist Danny Brower led to a hypothesis of the origin of the human mind that deals specifically with Kassandra's problem, writing:

> Such an animal would already have built-in reflex mechanisms for fear responses to dangerous or life-threatening situations. But this unconscious fear would now become a conscious one, a constant terror of knowing one is going to die, and that it could happen anytime, anywhere. In this model, selection would only favor the individual who attains full ToM [Theory of Mind] at about the same time as also achieving the ability to deny his or her mortality. This combination would be a very rare event. It is even possible that this was the defining moment

for the original speciation of behaviorally modern humans. This is the Rubicon that we humans seem to have crossed over.[30]

The argument offered in *Denial* is that if an animal like Kassandra were to be born with that combination of cognitive skills that leads to death wisdom (equivalent to what is referred to as "full ToM" in the quote on the previous page), then it would fail to survive because of the "extremely negative immediate consequences."[31] Essentially, it would lose its mind and be unable to sire any offspring at all (let alone survive its childhood). Only by evolving the ability to compartmentalize these thoughts of mortality (what Varki calls the *capacity for denial*) would an animal like Kassandra be able to remain sane enough to procreate.

What, then, are the evolutionary benefits to death wisdom? If it's such a potential liability that we can only explain its existence through a capacity for denying it, why was it so darn helpful to Kassandra that she became the dominant genetic line? Here's the answer: Death wisdom relies on cognitive skills that are hugely beneficial to the human ability to understand how the world works (e.g., mental time travel, episodic foresight, explicit knowledge of time). Our capacity for being able to ask why things happen, and thus make predictions and plans that can change the course of events, is part of our why specialist aptitude that we learned about in Chapter 1. Episodic foresight is clearly a cognitive capacity that is involved in this process. And since death wisdom is an unavoidable knock-on effect of episodic foresight, we simply cannot unlink death wisdom from our why specialist capacity. Natural selection appears to see the benefit in why specialism insofar as it has helped us proliferate. The same must then be true of episodic foresight and its companion death wisdom. So a clear benefit to death wisdom is its involvement in — or perhaps emergence from — other cognitive capacities that have allowed our species to outcompete all other hominids and most other mammals for domination of this planet.

It's also possible that death wisdom might have helped our species achieve success by bolstering our capacity for shared sociality. Far from being a bug in the system, or an unwanted knock-on effect, it might actually be a feature. The psychologist Ernest Becker won a Pulitzer for his book *The Denial of Death,* wherein he explains that much of human behavior — and most of our culture — is generated in response to our knowledge about our own deaths, and subsequent attempts to create something that is immortal, something that will live on after we have died, and thus has meaning and value.[32] Humans create systems of belief, and laws, and science so that we can find for ourselves what Becker described as "a feeling of primary value, of cosmic specialness, of ultimate usefulness to creation, of unshakable meaning." We build temples, skyscrapers, and multigenerational families in the hope that "the things that man creates in society are of lasting worth and meaning, that they outlive or outshine death and decay, that man and his products count." Ernest Becker makes a good case that death wisdom inspires us to create a plethora of immortality projects, some of which themselves might be a boon to our evolutionary fitness as they get transmitted down to future generations via culture. Things like science itself, which is driven as much by the individual scientists' desire for infamy as it is the pure love of knowledge.

Becker is right. There is no denying that death wisdom generates beautiful things that add value (and meaning) to the human condition. But it is precisely our faith in the importance of our cultural immortality projects and their absolute central role in our feelings of worth that brings out the worst in human behavior. Holy wars are fought between competing ideologies about the nature of the path to immortality. Genocide — like that masterminded by King Leopold II in Congo in consort with Christian missionaries — is committed in the name of our timeless gods (both theological and economic). Walk around any city on this planet and you will likely encounter statues of historical figures whose names and likeness we still know precisely because they dedicated their lives to achieving notoriety for all the wrong reasons. You can still find statues honoring Joseph Stalin, Nathan Bedford Forrest, and Cecil Rhodes. Many of these statues celebrate the lives of individuals who achieved fame through war, murder, and the subjugation of their fellow humans. Death wisdom does give us the drive to seek out immortality by generating art and beauty, but also — perhaps ironically — death.

There are other negative consequences to death wisdom from an evolutionary perspective. Aside from the previously stated immortality projects that have clearly gone awry (e.g., genocide), there are the everyday negative consequences of death wisdom. Things like depression, anxiety, and suicide. Although mood disorders have complex origins that can involve a huge number of causes (e.g., seasonal affective disorder, which can be triggered by changes in hormone levels due to lack of exposure to sunlight, or postpartum depression triggered by hormonal changes in a woman's body after giving birth), there is no doubt that our ability to contemplate our deaths can negatively impact our mood. So much so that feelings of nihilism, hopelessness, and thoughts of death are wrapped up in a depression diagnosis and are potential causes in and of themselves of suicide. There are currently 280 million people on this planet with depression. More than 700,000 people will die by suicide this year; it's the fourth leading cause of death in five- to twenty-nine-year-olds.[33] While death wisdom on its own is surely not the reason for these depression and suicide numbers, there is no doubt it is involved. Nietzsche himself is perhaps the classic example, having lived with lifelong depression while simultaneously grappling with the philosophical problem of nihilism. These things are surely inexorably linked.

I know from my life that I do not spend very much time contemplating my death. Occasionally, like my daughter, I have moments late at night when trying to fall asleep where the reality of death creeps into my mind and dread takes hold. But these thoughts are fleeting, soon replaced by song lyrics or tomorrow's to-do list. This is, I suspect, the reality for most humans. Just because we can contemplate our demise does not necessarily mean that we spend too much time actually doing it. This, then, is how our capacity for death denial keeps us sane. It allows us to ignore these morbid, intrusive thoughts just long enough so that we can get our laundry done.

Arguably on balance, the benefits of episodic foresight and why specialism outweigh the negative consequences of death wisdom. The simple fact that there are eight billion of us spread around this globe each having contemplated our deaths at some point suggests that death wisdom is manageable. As far as evolution is concerned, death wisdom is not problematic enough to have affected our success as a species.

But the day-to-day consequences of death wisdom really do suck. I believe that animals have a better relationship to death than we do. As we have seen in this chapter, many animals do know they can die. They know what death is. They are not ignorant enough to, as Nietzsche put it, "play in blissful blindness between the hedges of the past and future," as the previously mentioned quote from Nietzsche suggested. But despite this knowledge, they do not suffer as much as we do for the simple reason that they cannot imagine their deaths. A narwhal will never lament the specter of death like Nietzsche did. Had he been a narwhal, he would've been free from nihilistic dread. And had I been a narwhal, I would not have had to sit at my daughter's bedside watching her eyes fill with tears as she thought about her inevitable death. I would trade any of my beloved immortality projects to wipe the death wisdom curse from my daughter's mind.

Chapter 4

The Gay Albatross
Around Our Necks

The problem with human morality

We do not consider animals as moral beings. But do
you think that animals consider us as moral beings?
An animal which had the power of speech once
said: "Humanity is a prejudice from which we animals at least do not suffer."

— Nietzsche[1]

Hashizume Aihei was a soldier in the 6th Infantry Division of the imperial Japanese army. On March 8, 1868,
Hashizume's division was stationed in the seaside town
of Sakai (near Osaka) when soldiers from a French war-
ship anchored in the harbor — the *Dupleix* — came ashore.
This was only a year after the start of the Meiji Restora-
tion in Japan, a transition from a feudal system ruled

over by shoguns (military dictators) to a central imperial government that, for the first time in centuries, per-
mitted Westerners onto Japanese soil. It was the first
time the townspeople of Sakai had seen a foreigner, and
they were quite dismayed when the French soldiers began
casually sauntering through their sacred temples and
flirting with the locals. The French sailors' behavior was
exactly what you'd expect of a nineteenth-century Western seafarer on shore leave, but the Japanese considered
it a disgusting breach of decency. Hashizume and his
men were ordered to persuade the French soldiers to go
back to their boats, which was nigh impossible given the
language barrier. Frustrated, the Japanese soldiers took
action, grabbing and restraining one by binding his hands.
Thinking this was the start of a confrontation, the French
fled toward their boats, but one stole a Japanese military
flag as he ran past. The Japanese flagbearer, a firefighter
named Umekichi, ran after the French flag thief and
split his head open with an ax. In retaliation, the French
began shooting their pistols at Umekichi. Hashizume
and his fellow soldiers drew their rifles and returned
fire. The French were vastly outnumbered and out-
gunned, having intended only to explore the town (and
accost local women). They were wholly unprepared for
battle. After a brief volley of bullets, the Japanese had
killed sixteen French soldiers.

Given the new and still precarious relations between
them, diplomats from both sides were quick to quiet tem-
pers, preventing further bloodshed. The French insisted

that the Japanese military be held accountable for the deaths. They demanded an official apology, $150,000 USD in compensation, and the execution of twenty of the Japanese soldiers responsible for the massacre.

All seventy-three soldiers involved in the incident were interrogated, with twenty-nine men admitting that they had fired their weapons. All twenty-nine were willing to be executed in honor of their emperor. Since the French diplomats had asked for only twenty, the soldiers went to a temple where they drew straws to determine who would die. Hashizume made the cut. The nine soldiers who didn't make it were disappointed. They protested their fate, demanding to be executed alongside Hashizume and their fellow soldiers. Their request was denied.

It's at this part of the story where the question of what the correct moral path is depends entirely on your cultural background.

Hashizume and the other soldiers condemned to death accepted — even embraced — their fate, but they did not agree that they had violated any military code. After all, the French had fired first. What they wanted was an altered sentence: to die by ritual suicide — seppuku — instead of being executed. Doing so would elevate them to the status of samurai — the ultimate goal of any foot soldier. They were granted this request, which, in the eyes of the Japanese authorities, was a chance to surreptitiously humiliate the French and rain honor — not retribution — onto their condemned soldiers.

On March 16, 1868, Hashizume and the nineteen others were dressed in ceremonial white hakama and black haori and carried on palanquins (fancy covered litters) accompanied by hundreds of soldiers to a Buddhist temple. They were provided a last meal of fish and sake. Dignitaries from both nations were seated across from where seppuku would take place. Among them was the commander of the *Dupleix,* the fantastically named Abel-Nicolas Georges Henri Bergasse du Petit-Thouars, the senior French official on hand to verify that the Japanese would hold up their end of the deal.

One by one, the soldiers came forward where they calmly knelt on a tatami mat and plunged their sword into their belly, severing the superior mesenteric artery in their abdomen. While in agony, they bowed their heads and were then beheaded by their assistant. Seppuku is an ancient practice formalized over the course of seven hundred years of samurai history. This is the first time it had been witnessed by a non-Japanese person, and du Petit-Thouars was, to say the least, shocked. According to some accounts, du Petit-Thouars stood repeatedly during the ceremony, overcome by how impossibly calm these men were as they disemboweled themselves. Hashizume was twelfth in line and, just as he was about to begin seppuku, du Petit-Thouars demanded that the ceremony be stopped, decrying that the debt had been paid. He then gathered the remaining French dignitaries and hastily retreated to their ship.

For Hashizume, this was a huge dishonor. He was

being denied a righteous death — a chance to bring honor on himself and his emperor. Whereas du Petit-Thouars considered the stay an act of mercy, it was, for Hashizume, precisely the opposite. The remaining nine samurai were told, a few days later, that du Petit-Thouars had petitioned that their death sentences be revoked. This was such a blow to Hashizume that, upon hearing the news, he bit through his tongue in hopes that he might bleed to death. For Hashizume and the other men, the mercy shown by du Petit-Thouars was a fate worse than death.[2]

Let's consider the moral quandaries this story evokes. Was it justified in the first place for the French to demand executions as payment for the killing of their soldiers? Is the eye-for-an-eye system moral? Or are state-sanctioned executions inherently barbaric and amoral? Was du Petit-Thouars being merciful when he halted the ceremony? If so, merciful in whose eyes? Certainly not to the Japanese soldiers spared. Is honor by suicide an anachronistic moral code? As this story shows, answers to these moral questions vary depending on whom you ask, where they are from, and what century it is. Morality, while not necessarily wholly arbitrary, is largely culturally determined.

The fact that sociocultural and historical context has such an enormous influence on what we consider right or wrong behavior suggests that our moral sense is not a monolithic code bestowed upon us by external, supernatural forces. It appears more like a set of inherited prescripts that get tweaked by culture. If that's true, then our capacity for morality is something that evolved like any other cognitive trait. At least, that's what it looks like to scientists studying animal behavior. The primatologist Frans de Waal has published many amazing books on the subject of social complexity in animals, and has popularized the idea of the bottom-up approach to the evolution of human morality. This proposes that human morality (including religiosity) is not handed down to us by god(s). Nor is it derived exclusively from high-level thinking about the nature of right and wrong. It is instead a natural outcropping (shaped by evolution) of behavior and cognition that is common to all social animals. "The moral law is not imposed from above or derived from well-reasoned principles," writes de Waal in *The Bonobo and the Atheist*, "rather it arises from ingrained values that have been there since the beginning of time."[3]

Consider, for example, how other primate species fueled by ancient, ingrained values would handle social conflict reminiscent of the Sakai incident. Such as the stump-tailed macaque, an old-world monkey that lives across the sea from Japan in southeast Asia. Like most primates, conflict is a normal part of their social world. Fights determine who's in charge and where each sits on the social ladder. Stump-tailed macaques live in groups of up to sixty individuals, with the alpha male being the main protector of the group, and the one who gets exclusive rights to mate with the females and sire offspring.

Alpha males are occasionally challenged by younger males and must assert their dominance. Imagine, then, a hypothetical scenario where a young male has wandered over to where the alpha male is busy grooming a female. The young male sits down and starts running his fingers through the female's fur, looking for mites. Given his status, it's the alpha who has priority for grooming this female, so this intrusion simply won't stand. The alpha reprimands the precocious young male by smacking him upside the head. In order to make amends, the young male turns around and presents his hindquarters to the alpha male — wiggling his bottom near his face. The alpha recognizes this is an act of contrition, and grabs hold of the young male's bottom, hugging and holding on to it for a few moments. This is a signal that their relationship has been restored and all is well. The lesson here being that both animals knew that some sort of rule had been violated, and something had to be done to clarify who was in charge.[4]

Social animals (like macaques) live by codes that dictate how they should and should not behave within their social worlds. Scientists call these codes animal *norms*. Humans have norms that guide our actions, too, as we will learn. But humans also have additional codes that guide our actions in the form of morals. Unlike norms, morals tell us not just that we should behave a certain way, but *why* we should. Hashizume believed that he should perform seppuku *because* it honors the emperor and would allow him to die a samurai, for example. Du

Petit-Thouars believed he should halt the execution *because* it was creating unnecessary suffering. Unlike norms, which are unspoken rules operating in the background, moral positions have been explicitly considered, evaluated, and decided upon by either the individual, society/culture, or perhaps even our gods.

This chapter is dedicated to showing how the human cognitive skills that we've encountered so far in this book — like why specialism, death wisdom, theory of mind — have molded the human moral sense from the clay of animal normativity. But I will also show that it is in fact animals that usually hold the ethical high ground despite lacking the capacity for full-blown human moral thinking. You see, human moral reasoning often leads to more death, violence, and destruction than we find in the normative behavior of nonhuman animals. Which is why human morality, as I will argue, kind of sucks.

Consider how the Sakai incident might have been resolved with macaque-style restorative justice. Imagine the French acknowledging that it was the Japanese who had a right to protect their village due to their alpha-male-like status, and that it was du Petit-Thouars who would need to atone for his troops' poor behavior while on shore leave. As the samurai seated around the outdoor pavilion looked on, du Petit-Thouars, dressed in military regalia, would walk over to a kneeling Hashizume and squat in front of him with his keister in the air. Hashizume would then grab du Petit-Thouars's bottom and hold it tightly in his arms for a few minutes while everyone in the crowd nodded along with appreciation. Nobody would have to die. There would be no concept of honor or politically motivated retribution. Only reconciliation, and the heartwarming image of a samurai hugging a Frenchman's bottom.

Bottoms up

All animals, including humans, appear to live and die by implicit, unexamined, and unspoken rules. Scientists and philosophers use the word *norms* to label the implicit rules determining which behaviors are allowed or expected within an animal's social world. The philosophers Kristin Andrews and Evan Westra at York University use the term *normative regularity* to describe the kind of norm-based system that governs animal societies, which they define as "a socially maintained pattern of behavioral conformity within a community."[5]

These patterns of conformity that Andrews and Westra highlight are readily apparent to anyone who spends time watching animals. My chickens, for example, have clear patterns of behavior concerning which of them gets first access to the spaghetti that I throw over their fence. Shadow, who's far up the pecking order, is always the first one to grab any food I toss over. Dr. Becky, on the other hand, is near the bottom of the social order, and will hover near the outskirts of the group. If Dr. Becky should try to muscle her way in to grab some spaghetti before her turn, she will get pecked by Shadow.

Dr. Becky will have violated a norm about who gets to eat first. My chickens have a system for determining what each other should and should not do when it comes to eating first (and the consequences of violating those norms) to maintain patterns of conformity (i.e., the pecking order) for the group.

Westra explained to me by email that norms are not synonymous with rules since "in practice, it's pretty hard to tell what rule — if any — an animal is actually following when it behaves a certain way," and that "a number of philosophers and cognitive scientists actually think that feeling is a more central part of social norms than actually having rules." When norms are violated, there are often consequences in the form of negative emotions (for both the violator and the violated), and sometimes active punishment. Animals feel pressure to conform to norms in the form of anxiety or discomfort or even anger if a norm is violated. Norm violations usually result in behaviors that help reestablish the status quo to make those negative emotions go away, like Shadow pecking Dr. Becky, or the bottom-holding reconciliation technique favored by macaques. The pressure that animals feel to conform to norms, and the consequences they experience for violating them in the form of negative emotions, is what maintains the social structure for all animal societies.

Animals like chickens do not need much in the way of complex cognition for these social norms to both crop up and guide their actions through negative emotions. Chickens do not need theory of mind in order to guess what the other chickens might know about the pecking order. Nor do my chickens need causal inference to ruminate on the reasons why Dr. Becky should wait to eat last, and whether this is fair or just. Most norms work like this for animals; patterns of behavior guided by emotions that are otherwise unconsidered. In fact, most norms work like this for humans, too.

Human behavior is governed by norms that we internalize but that are not taught to us explicitly. Because they are unexamined and untaught, and thus not framed by ideas of good/bad or right/wrong, they are not elevated to the level of morals. Consider the norm involved with whether it's acceptable to wipe someone else's face. Chances are you live in a society where it would be unacceptable to walk up to a stranger on the street with a napkin in your hand and wipe food from the corner of their mouth. This is a rather intimate behavior that we reserve for our children and loved ones and maybe a close friend, but not at all something we do with strangers. No one taught you this, yet you respect this rule all the same. And chances are you had never even thought or read about this face-wiping rule before now, proving that you had internalized the rule before I even mentioned it. You would simply feel uncomfortable trying to wipe a stranger's face with a napkin. That's the classic nature of a norm: an unspoken rule guiding your behavior by manipulating your emotions.

There are many types of emotions lurking in the

minds of animals (including humans) that help generate normative behavior. And some are far more complex than just feeling uncomfortable.[6] Consider the emotion of *equity*. When scientists scanned the brains of people asked to make a decision about distributing food to hungry children, regions of the brain involved in emotional response — the insular cortex — were activated when food was distributed unfairly.[7] "Given the involvement of the insular cortex in emotions and fairness judgments," lead author Ming Hsu told ABC News, "we conclude that emotions are underlying equity judgments."[8] In other words, equity and fairness are not high-level moral judgments in the human brain, but emotion-driven norms lurking in the periphery of our consciousness. Which is why it's no surprise that we find equity and fairness present in the minds of other animals.

Perhaps the most famous experiment showing the presence of fairness in animals was conducted by Sarah Brosnan and Frans de Waal. They tested a group of capuchin monkeys for their sensitivity to social inequality by offering them different food rewards for completing the same task. In his 2011 TED Talk, de Waal played a video for the audience that showed two female monkeys (Lance and Winter) in side-by-side cages. A researcher places a rock in Lance's cage, which she hands back to the researcher, receiving a slice of cucumber as a reward. The researcher then places a rock in Winter's cage, which she hands back and receives a grape as a reward. Capuchins vastly prefer grapes to cucumbers, and Lance watches this exchange with interest. The researcher again places a rock in Lance's cage and again gives Lance a cucumber in return. Lance tastes it, realizes it is a cucumber and not a grape, and then throws it violently back at the researcher. She then bangs angrily on the table and rattles her cage. This is evidence that Lance felt as if it was unfair that she was given the lesser food reward for the same task. Lance was responding to the violation of a fairness norm.

This, however, does not mean that Lance necessarily has a sense of morality. Clearly, a sense of fairness leading to moral codes is the bedrock upon which human justice and legal systems are built. It is what drove the French and Japanese to behave the way they did during the Sakai incident. But a subconscious notion of fairness is but a shadow of the kind of moral complexity found in, for example, the samurai code. "This is because sentiments do not suffice," argues de Waal. "We strive for a logically coherent system and have debates about how the death penalty fits arguments for the sanctity of life, or whether an unchosen sexual orientation can be morally wrong. These debates are uniquely human. This is what sets human morality apart: a move toward universal standards combined with an elaborate system of justification, monitoring, and punishment."[9]

Unlike animals, humans have formal, explicit rules for "right" and "wrong" with elaborate and well-considered justifications. And, unlike animals, we are constantly adjusting what we consider right and wrong as our cultures and societies evolve. We derive these formal ideas from philosophical and religious discussions about the nature of morality and ethics. Consider the many reasons we can give for why it's wrong to eat pigs. A Judeo-Christian religious leader might, for example, argue that it is wrong to eat pigs because the Bible considers them an "unclean" animal.[10] An abolitionist philosopher — one that argues that all animal use of any kind is inherently wrong — might argue that it's wrong to eat pigs because sentient nonhuman animals have an inherent right to not be treated as property. A lawmaker might decide that eating pigs is fine, but only if they have been slaughtered at a sanctioned abattoir by a licensed butcher, and that the meat had been processed according to relevant health codes. All of these moral and legal systems denoting right and wrong (and the definitions of *right* and *wrong* themselves) depend largely on the human capacity to hold these ideas in our conscious minds, and formalize them via the medium of language.

How, then, did *Homo sapiens* create our moral system from the normative systems we find in other animals? Are cognitive skills like language necessary? In his book *A Natural History of Human Morality,* the developmental psychologist Michael Tomasello describes human morality as "a form of cooperation" that emerged as humans "adapted to new and species-unique forms of social interaction and organization," resulting in *Homo sapiens* becoming an "ultracooperative primate."[11] For

Tomasello, the evolution of this cooperation-based morality did not initially rely on language as much as it did
the precursors of theory of mind. He imagines a period
in our evolutionary history — predating the appearance
of our ancestors we saw around Lake Baringo in Chapter 1 — when ancient hominids started doing something
novel: hunting together in pairs. To hunt with a partner
requires an understanding that the other person has a
goal that is the same as yours (e.g., kill an antelope). This
understanding (called *joint intentionality*) where you
understand the goals of another creature is a precursor
to theory of mind (which gives you an understanding
of beliefs and not just goals). There is evidence that
some nonhuman species — like chimpanzees — engage
in hunting practices that involve joint intentionality
along these lines.[12] In Tomasello's imagined scenario, a
sense of "we" emerges from these scenarios where each
partner had clear expectations for how the other partner
ought to act in order to collaborate and hunt the antelope. Rules and norms begin to crop up helping us determine, for example, the correct way to divvy up the meat
after a kill so both members of the "we" are fairly
rewarded for their contribution to the hunt.

Once humans began gathering in larger groups
100,000 years ago, the next phase of human moral evolution began: the transition from joint intentionality to
collective intentionality. The "we" of the two-person
hunting pair was, at some point in our evolutionary history, upgraded to the "us" of the tribe. Our ancestors

were able to make better guesses as to what one another were thinking (via a fully developed theory of mind) and could use language to probe one another's thoughts and coordinate behavior on large scales. Once human groups began competing (and fighting) with other human groups, this tribal sense of "us" and "them" spawned a new set of rules about what others "ought" to be doing if they are to remain a member of "us." Coupled with language, you can see how this collective intentionality would spawn formal rules and laws governing the behavior of individuals within a large social group.

But language and theory of mind are not the only ingredients that helped generate the human moral sense as our societies grew. Humans, unlike animals, can ponder the very nature and origin of those normative emotions bubbling up from within our minds and ask ourselves not only where they come from, but why they are there in the first place. I daresay that most humans on this planet would disagree with the idea that norms are ancient evolutionary adaptations shared by many species to help regulate social interactions. Most would suggest the norms that generate our moral behavior are put in our minds by a supernatural entity of some kind. Or maybe there exists a universal moral code that is part of the fabric of existence that our species alone has the mental tools to contemplate. These conclusions are natural outcroppings of our why specialist nature. Combine this line of inquiry with our death wisdom and you have the question of "why do you have to die?," which is intimately tied to the problem of how we should behave while we're alive in case it impacts what happens to us in the afterlife. The most common answer to these questions involves a religious explanation, like heaven and hell, samsara, etc. Even non-supernatural explanations as to the origins and value of morality and how to live a good life are all products of our why specialist thinking. Philosophers have been generating formalized moral systems to help guide our behavior for millennia. They are all based on the application of systematized thinking to the problem of which behaviors are good or bad, and why we should choose one action over another.

The peculiarity of human moral behavior lies in its ability to be formalized, analyzed, revised, and propagated on a large scale. This gives us, in theory, a more sophisticated take on the concept of right and wrong compared to animals, who are stuck with a finite set of emotions generating behavioral norms (but not explicit rules or laws) on a much smaller scale. You could argue that these human cognitive peculiarities made us an advanced moral animal. Or, as Tomasello writes, results in humans being "the only moral one." But I think the way in which humans behave in deference to their moral thinking results in truly bonkers behavior (from an evolutionary perspective) and might in fact make us *less* moral than other species. If, that is, we define *moral* as the ability to produce beneficial behavior and minimize pain and suffering. To make this point, all I need to do is read the current headlines here in Canada.

136

It became necessary to destroy the town to save it

Sir John Alexander Macdonald, the first prime minister of Canada, believed that white Western culture was superior to all other cultures, and that the integration of the Indigenous peoples of Canada into Western society was a noble cause if not a moral imperative. Under his leadership, the Canadian government established the Indian Act of 1876, which outlined the government's approach to assimilating First Nations people into Western European culture, including the banning of indigenous religious and cultural ceremonies.

But the government felt they needed a more proactive system to ensure assimilation occurred quickly. An obvious place to start would be the reeducation of Indigenous youth. With this in mind, the residential school system was authorized in 1883, with the goal of "separating Aboriginal children from their families, in order to minimize and weaken family ties and cultural linkages, and to indoctrinate children into a new culture — the culture of the legally dominant Euro-Christian Canadian society."[13] Sir John Alexander Macdonald had this to say about the establishment of the residential schools when speaking to the House of Commons in 1883:

> When the school is on the reserve the child lives with its parents, who are savages; he is surrounded by savages, and though he may learn to read and

137

write, his habits and training and mode of thought are Indian. He is simply a savage who can read and write. It has been strongly pressed on myself, as the head of the Department, that Indian children should be withdrawn as much as possible from the parental influence, and the only way to do that would be to put them in central training industrial schools where they will acquire the habits and modes of thought of white men.

The Canadian residential school systems were funded by the federal government, but run by the Roman Catholic, Anglican, Methodist, Presbyterian, and the United churches of Canada. By 1896, there were forty schools across Canada. In 1920, attendance was made mandatory for all Indigenous children ages seven to sixteen. There are endless heartbreaking stories of children as young as four or five being forcibly removed from their homes and taken to residential schools thousands of miles away. Isaac Daniels, a residential school survivor, explained what happened to him in 1945 at his home on the James Smith Reserve in Saskatchewan when an "Indian agent" (a federal government representative) came to take him to a residential school:

I didn't understand a word, 'cause I spoke Cree. Cree was the main language in our family. So, so my dad was kind of angry. I kept seeing him pointing to that Indian agent. So that night we were going to bed, it was just a one-room shack we all lived in, and I heard my dad talking to my mom there, and he was kind of crying, but he was talking in Cree now. He said that, "It's either residential school for my boys, or I go to jail." He said that in Cree. So, I overheard him. So I said the next morning, we all got up, and I said, "Well, I'm going to residential school," 'cause I didn't want my dad to go to jail.

Once at the schools, siblings were separated (to further break them of family ties), and they were forbidden from speaking their native languages. Conditions at the schools were deplorable: drafty, cold, cramped, with poor sanitation, and inadequate access to food and water. Disease was rampant, as was physical and sexual abuse at the hands of the church leaders and school employees. A government report stated that "the failure to develop, implement, and monitor effective discipline sent an unspoken message that there were no real limits on what could be done to Aboriginal children within the walls of a residential school. The door had been opened early to an appalling level of physical and sexual abuse of students, and it remained open throughout the existence of the system."[14]

In the 1956–57 school year, residential schools saw peak enrollment at 11,539 children. All in all, 150,000 children attended residential schools in Canada until the last school was closed in 1996. In the hundred-plus years of the residential school system, the number of children who died in them was a minimum of 3,200. Most recorded deaths were caused by tuberculosis, but the majority of deaths (51 percent) had no specific cause listed. The rates of death and disease at the schools far exceeded the national averages at the time. Children who died at the schools were rarely sent home to their families for burial. Instead, they were buried in graves (often unmarked) on school grounds.

The horrors of the Canadian Indian residential school system were laid bare in a 2015 report from the Truth and Reconciliation Commission (TRC). The TRC was established as part of a deal negotiated after a successful class-action lawsuit against the Canadian federal government filed by a group of more than seven thousand residential school survivors. According to the TRC report, the Canadian government has had the goal of cultural genocide from its first interactions with the Indigenous peoples of Canada. The TRC report notes that "it was not uncommon for principals, in their annual reports, to state that a specific number of students had died in the previous year, but not to name them." When the schools eventually closed, the bodies of these nameless children were forgotten. After decades of pleas from First Nations, the sites are only now being investigated, and the bodies (and the names) of these children are finally being recovered.

On May 27, 2021, a ground-penetrating radar specialist working for the Tk'emlúps te Secwépemc First Nation in Kamloops, British Columbia, released a preliminary report, which exposed the remains of 215 children found on the grounds of the former Kamloops Indian Residential School. A month later, 751 unmarked graves were found at the former site of the Marieval Indian Residential School in Marieval, Saskatchewan. As of this writing in the summer of 2021, Canadian news media are revealing the atrocities committed at these residential schools, and the nation is grappling with the reality that the government — working in close contact with a number of Christian churches — is responsible for committing cultural genocide.

These atrocities are, at their root, products of moral reasoning. Sir John Alexander Macdonald viewed the residential school as a moral imperative, the best solution for bringing Indigenous children in line with modern Western values. The churches were operating under a similar imperative, albeit one derived directly from their scriptural interpretations. In the New Testament, Jesus spoke to his disciplines about God's wish to spread the news about his teachings. In Matthew 28:19–20, Jesus said: "Go therefore and make disciples of all nations, baptizing them in the name of the Father and of the Son and of the Holy Spirit, and teaching them to obey everything that I have commanded you." The missionary work that started in Canada in the seventeenth century and that carried on in the residential schools until they closed in 1996 was based on these divine commandments. Consider the words of Reverend Samuel Rose, principal of the Mount Elgin residential school, writing about the need to break the ties his young Chippewa students had with their culture:

> This class is to spring a generation, who will either perpetuate the manners and customs of their ancestors, or being intellectually, morally and religiously elevated, take their stand among the improved, intelligent nations of the earth, their part in the great drama of the world's doing; or of want of necessary qualifications, to take their place and perform their part, be despised and pushed off the stage of action and ceased to be![15]

This is divine moral reasoning that justified cultural genocide.

All churches involved in the residential-school programs in Canada have issued apologies for their involvement in this horrid practice. The Catholic Church, which operated 70 percent of the residential schools, did not issue an apology until April of 2022, after First Nations, Inuit, and Métis delegates traveled to Rome to ask Pope Francis to acknowledge and apologize for the Church's role in Canada's residential-school system. One can only speculate as to the hesitation to apologize, but it might well come down to the possibility that the Church did not believe that it had done anything wrong. Some church leaders argue as much. Following the news of the discovery of the bodies of children on the grounds of the residential school at Kamloops, a Catholic priest in Mississauga, Ontario, released a YouTube video of his sermon wherein he said, "Two-thirds of the country is blaming the church, which we love, for the tragedies that occurred [at Kamloops]. I presume the same number would thank the church for the good done in those schools, but of course, that question was never asked and we are not allowed to even say that good was done there."[16]

This example underscores the dark reality of the human moral capacity: We, as a species, can justify — on moral grounds — genocide. Not just cultural genocide, but the murder of entire populations and racial groups, including children. During the Nuremburg trial of Nazi war criminals, the SS leader Otto Ohlendorf calmly explained why he was justified in overseeing the murder of thousands of Jewish children. "I believe that it is very simple to explain if one starts from the fact that [the Führer's] order not only tried to achieve security, but *permanent* security, lest the children grow up and inevitably, being the children of parents who had been killed, they would constitute a danger no smaller than that of the parents."[17] In other words, in order to ensure the safety of future generations of Germans, Jewish children had to be eliminated lest they grow up to resent the Nazis for murdering their parents. It is a logical moral position to take insofar as it was an attempt to minimize societal pain and suffering in the long term, but so unbelievably repugnant and horrifying that we still recoil in horror at the Nazis' ability to justify their actions.

From the moment Canadian residential schools were first established, many political and religious leaders believed that they — like the Nazis — were a force for good. That the hardships and deaths of Indigenous children were worth it in the end. Consider the chilling words about the value of these schools written by Duncan Campbell Scott, deputy superintendent general of Indian affairs from 1913 until 1932:

> It is readily acknowledged that Indian children lose their natural resistance to illness by habitating so closely in these schools, and that they die at a much higher rate than in their villages. But this alone does not justify a change in the policy of this Department, which is being geared towards the final solution of our Indian Problem.[18]

This kind of moral reasoning is only possible with human-style cognition. In contrast, animal behavior within a given species' social group — guided by normativity — is typically far less violent and destructive, as I will show in the next section. While there are examples of things such as infanticide for animals (like we see in our great ape cousins or dolphins), or within-group violence leading to the death of individuals, animals do not have the cognitive capacity to systematically kill entire subgroups of their same-species populations resulting from a formal claim to moral authority.

The wisdom of gay albatrosses

Outside of humans, the best (worst?) example of repugnant same-species violence is found in chimpanzees. When compared to other nonhuman great apes, chimpanzees are notoriously bloodthirsty. I mean that literally. Rival chimpanzee groups defending their territories will engage in open battle where they will occasionally beat one another to death. But they also conduct clandestine raids into enemy territory, targeting rival males to kill. In the book *Demonic Males: Apes and the Origins of Human Violence,* primatologist Richard W. Wrangham and science writer Dale Peterson note that these raids are "marked by a gratuitous cruelty — tearing off pieces of skin, for example, twisting limbs until they break, and drinking a victim's blood — reminiscent of acts that among humans are regarded as unspeakable crimes during peacetime and atrocities during war."[19]

The primatologist Sarah Blaffer Hrdy describes the violent nature of chimpanzees in the opening pages of her 2011 book, *Mothers and Others: The Evolutionary Origins of Mutual Understanding.*[20] Humans, she notes, can spend hours crowded together in an airplane without resorting to violence, even when faced with rude passengers and crying babies. "What if I were traveling with a planeload of chimpanzees?" she asks. "Any one of us would be lucky to disembark with all ten fingers and toes still attached, with the baby still breathing and unmaimed. Bloody earlobes and other appendages would litter the aisles." In other words, chimpanzees are terribly violent and often outright murderous, and they inflict this upon one another.

But even this behavior pales in comparison to the kind of violence that humans exhibit, and our moral reasoning justifies it. Chimpanzees have never been observed killing every individual (males and females, juveniles and newborns) within a rival group; the unspoken behavioral rule or norm that chimpanzees live by when they battle is to only remove a select few individuals (usually the adult males) so as to make the rival group less of a threat. Perhaps, if they had the humanlike cognitive abilities that allowed them to formalize their norms into morals, these raids would be far more expansive and destructive. But they don't. In contrast, when humans go to battle, they justify the killing of entire cities filled with noncombatants (including children) if it serves the greater (morally defensible) goal of winning the war in order to bring about peace. This is how we ended up with the infamous quote, "It became necessary to destroy the town to save it," spoken by a US Army major when justifying the bombing of Bến Tre during the Vietnam War despite there being children in the town.[21] Like so many human moral decisions, the Army's decision to kill civilians emerged from our unique capacity for moral reasoning (i.e., the ability to formalize, analyze, revise, and propagate normative behavior on a large scale), a skill that chimpanzees lack, and the reason that even our most violent animal cousins are still less violent than us. While it's entirely true that the human capacity for cooperation is why, as Sarah Blaffer Hrdy argues in *Mothers and Others,* "face-to-face killings are a much harder sell for humans than for chimpanzees," and why, despite 1.6 billion airline passengers every year, "no dismemberments have been reported yet," it is also this human capacity for cooperation that gives humans (but not chimpanzees) the ability to bomb the children of Bến Tre and establish Indian residential schools.[22]

But to drive my point home that humans often wind up with unnecessarily violent behavioral norms due to our complex ability for moral reasoning, I don't want to talk about war. I want to talk about homosexuality. In the introduction to the book *The Biology of Homosexuality,* the biologist Jacques Balthazart writes that "homosexuality in humans is to a very large extent, if not exclusively, determined by biological factors acting prenatally or soon after birth." In other words, people's sexual orientation is largely determined at birth. He arrives at this conclusion through the study of same-sex sexual behavior in animals, where there is a mountain of evidence showing that not only is homosexuality not unique to humans, but it's rather the norm for most animal species. This is old news for scientists studying animal behavior and biology, which is why Balthazart writes, "Scientists reading this book will think, 'We have heard all this before.'...But somehow that information has either not made its way into the world outside the laboratory or has not been presented in a sufficiently definitive matter to affect the general population's view on the matter."

He's right. I'm surprised at the number of people I talk to about animal behavior that are shocked at how common homosexual behavior is in the animal kingdom. I often point gay animal skeptics to *Biological Exuberance* by Bruce Bagemihl — a 1999 book detailing more than three hundred different animal species that engage in a diverse array of behaviors that fall under the umbrella of homosexuality. Everything from same-sex sex, affection, pair bonds, and parenting. It might seem odd that homosexuality should be so widespread given that evolution is based on the need for animals to produce offspring. This is often a topic broached by anti-gay groups hoping to (misguidedly) show that same-sex behavior is not "natural." But the literature on animal homosexuality shows that same-sex sexual behavior in a given species does not negatively impact a species' reproductive rates, so it's a non-issue. Take the example of the Laysan albatross. This species of giant bird forms life-long pair bonds — where two individuals stay together for life, mating and raising offspring together over the course of many decades. Some of these lifelong pair-bonds are between same-sex couples. In one study of Laysan albatrosses living on Oahu, one-third of the life-long pairs were female same-sex couples.[23] In many of these cases, however, one or both females would mate with a male at some point, resulting in fertilized eggs that the female pairs raised together. Many of the cases of homosexuality in the animal kingdom work like this, where same-sex behaviors are just part of an individual's typical behavioral repertoire, and reproduction still occurs to ensure species survival. Bonobos are perhaps the best example: Individuals engage in sex between same- and opposite-sex partners on a regular basis, resulting in lots of gayness, but also lots of babies.

Exclusive attraction to members of the same sex is rarer, but not unheard of. In domestic sheep, it's estimated that 10 percent of rams (the males) are only interested in mating with other rams.[24] Researchers studying this phenomenon found that these gay rams had differences in their brains — a thicker cluster of neurons in part of their hypothalamus — when compared to straight sheep. The reason for the differences being the relative amount of estrogen levels that the developing ram was exposed to before birth. In other words, as Balthazart argues in his book, these rams were born gay. All this to say that there's nothing particularly unusual or controversial about (inborn) gayness in the animal kingdom.

Despite the frequency with which it crops up, same-sex attraction does not threaten the survival of the hundreds of species for which homosexuality has been observed. Which is why no animal species seems to have evolved any social norms around punishing individuals for engaging in same-sex acts. In other words, while same-sex attraction is not unique to humans, homophobia is.

Of course, there are many past and present cultures where homosexuality is normalized, accepted, and even embraced. Throughout most of Japanese history, for example, same-sex relationships have not been stigmatized, and stories of male-male love and sex have long been associated with the samurai warrior class,[25] and would've been something Hashizume Aihei and his fellow samurai would've found entirely uncontroversial. But in many modern cultures — and especially Western European, Middle Eastern, and African cultures with Judeo-Christian roots — homosexuality is not just socially unacceptable or controversial, but illegal and punishable by death. Iran's Islamic Penal Code — enacted after the Islamic revolution of 1979 — declares gay sex between men a capital offense, penalized by execution. A Pew Research Center poll from 2013 found that many Middle Eastern countries have negative views of homosexuality, with 97 percent of people in Jordan, 95 percent in Egypt, and 80 percent in Lebanon believing that homosexuality "should be rejected."[26] Even in current Western countries ostensibly tolerant of LGBTQ people, anti-gay sentiment abounds, rooted in Judeo-Christian values. Conversion therapy — an attempt to change people's unwanted and "unnatural" sexual orientation through various forms of "therapy" — is often aimed at minors, and is legal in most parts of the United States. It is often administered by Christian faith-based therapists, even though, according to a 2009 report by the American Psychological Association Task Force, "results of scientifically valid research indicate that it is unlikely that individuals will be able to reduce same-sex attractions or increase other-sex sexual attractions through [conversion therapy]."[27]

It's not the case that this moral rejection of homosexuality always has religious origins. The Nazis — famously secular — did not approve of homosexuality (especially male homosexuality) for the simple reason that it deviated from the norm, and anything abnormal was simply not fit for inclusion in the Third Reich. Subsequently, more than 100,000 gay men were arrested, and tens of thousands were executed in concentration camps.

The reality is that, in recent history, millions of humans around the globe have suffered violence or death because of anti-gay sentiment. LGBTQ people are four times more likely than the general population to be the victims of violent crime, and that's just in the US, where homosexual behavior is no longer criminalized, and where corporations like McDonald's proudly fly rainbow flags during Pride Month.[28] One can only speculate what the rates of violence must be in countries like Russia (which does not compile data on homophobic attacks), where a 2018 survey found that 63 percent of Russians believed that gays were conspiring to "destroy the spiritual values generated by Russians, through the propaganda of nontraditional sexual relations,"[29] and one in five Russians believed that gays should be "eliminated."[30] And all this despite the fact that homosexuality is just as common in humans as it is in other species. Around 4 percent of people in the US self-identify as lesbian, gay, bisexual, or transgender,[31] while more than 8 percent of people in the report having engaged in same-sex sexual behavior, and 11 percent acknowledge at least some attraction to the opposite sex.[32] These numbers are right on par with sheep, but significantly *lower* than the same-sex activity found in bonobos.

The conclusion here is that humans, through our complex capacity for moral thinking, have taken something that does not constitute a normative problem for any other species and turned it into an issue for which we can justify marginalization, criminalization, execution, and even genocide. This is, I argue, a case of animals having a far superior — that is, less violent and destructive — normative system for dealing with difference than almost all human cultures. Homosexuality is quite clearly not just normal in the animal world, but entirely non-destructive. Maybe even beneficial for maintaining animal societies. Why, then, are humans uniquely homophobic? It's a mystery that can only be solved if you understand how we can reason ourselves into a corner via our capacity for moral thinking. A handful of cultures and religions have convinced themselves that homosexuality is a moral problem, and millions of our fellow humans must suffer because of it. Not only does anti-gay sentiment have no real counterpart in the behavior of any other species, but it actively creates barriers to our species' success. It not only sows societal discord but leads to the suffering of a large swath of the human population. What biological benefit has been given to our species through our bizarre moral posturing around the non-problem "problem" of homosexuality? Precisely none. It is a sad testament to the cruelty of human moral reasoning.

Losing our moral authority

The history of our species is the story of the moral justification of violent acts resulting in the pain, suffering, and deaths for billions of our fellow humans who fall into the category of "other." That could be the Indigenous peoples of Canada, the LGBTQ community, Jews, Blacks, the disabled, women, etc. In contrast, most animal norms exist to maintain a social equilibrium that minimizes the need for pain, suffering, and death. If we operate from the base principle that pain, suffering, and death is generally a bad thing, then it seems as if animals have the right idea (and the higher moral ground) most of the time. But does this mean that human morality is "bad" in the evolutionary sense? Could it be the case that our capacity for moral reasoning — our philosophy, religions, and legal structures — is precisely the thing that gave our species the edge these past few millennia? The thing that has helped us organize our societies and spread across the globe in our great civilizations?

I don't think it was our moral capacity *per se* that was responsible for our success, but the other components of the human mind that gave us the ability to coordinate our efforts, like language and theory of mind. And it was our why specialism that did the heavy lifting when it came to divining the nature of the physical universe and the biological world, giving us the technological know-how that put our species on the map. Human morality, in contrast, wasn't necessary for any of this. As I've been arguing, I think we would've been better off without the ability to turn our ancient primate norms into absurd and destructive moral rules that gave us things like residential schools and anti-LGBTQ legislation. But you can't unlink these things. You cannot have that laundry list of positive cognitive skills without the negative consequences. Human moral reasoning was unavoidable. But that doesn't necessarily make it *good,* in an evolutionary sense. Human moral reasoning might be a bug and not a feature — an evolutionary spandrel that cropped up as our unique cognitive skills blossomed, but not itself a trait that natural selection selected for. Humans might currently be succeeding as a species not because of, but despite, our moral aptitude. We have taken this universal normative system that governs and constrains social behavior for most animals to weird extremes. Animals, with their less sophisticated normative systems, are the ones living the good life.

Chapter 5

The Mystery of the Happy Bee

It's time to talk about the "c" word

What do I care about the purring of one who cannot love, like the cat?

— Nietzsche[1]

With autumn approaching and daily temperatures beginning to drop, my honeybees are beginning their final preparations for winter. I've kept bees for the past three years and have grown accustomed to their end-of-season drama. The nectar collecting season is almost over, and they are now busy drying out the last of the honey for storage during the winter months. This will be their only food source until the dandelions start blooming again in March. To avoid the risk of starvation and ensure that there's enough honey to go around, they begin downsizing their population. They need just enough bees in the colony — maybe forty thousand — to keep themselves warm, but not so many that they burn through their food stores before spring. Which means September is the time to get rid of the freeloaders. In other words, the drones.

Drones are male honeybees whose sole purpose is to mate with new queens from other colonies. They are larger and fatter than the female worker bees, with big goofy eyes that help them spot other drones and virgin queens. They don't have stingers, and so can't defend the hive. In fact, they can't do much of anything other than mate. They don't clean the hive, make honeycomb, or look after larvae. Their tongues are short, so they are unable to collect nectar from flowers. They even have a hard time licking the honey out of the honeycombs, so female workers must place food directly into their mouths. Thus, during winter, drones are high maintenance and low value. Which is why, when September arrives, the female workers round up all the drones, drag them to the front entrance of the hive, and push them out. If they try to come back in, they are attacked or killed. Since they can't feed themselves, it won't be long before they starve or freeze to death. This time of year, the fronts of my hives are covered in banished and bewildered drones.

It's quite a tragic — but utterly natural — state of affairs, and I can't help but pity these poor guys. Lately, I have taken to collecting the hapless drones and putting them in a little cardboard box on my deck. I put some honey in there for them so they can try to feed themselves one last time before their inevitable death. I want to give them one final moment of happiness.

Last week, I showed my drone collection to my friend Andrea who is always amused by my animal escapades. "This seems like a lot of work for no reason," she said. "You're not really making them 'happier.' It's not like they're conscious. They don't appreciate all this effort."

"I'm not sure I agree with that," I said. "Out of curiosity, what animals do you think are conscious? Is Clover conscious?" Clover is Andrea's new border collie — a boisterous puppy who was staring intently at the chickens behind my fence.

"Yes, I think so," replied Andrea.

"What about those chickens?"

"Hmmm. Chickens? I'm not sure. No? If they are, they're a lot less conscious than Clover. But these bees aren't conscious. They're not self-aware. Insects just run on instinct."

"Would it surprise you to learn," I said, "that many scientists and philosophers would argue that these little drones are, in fact, conscious?"

"What? That's absurd. How on earth could they possibly make that argument?"

It's a good question.

What is consciousness?

Consciousness has always been considered one of the things that separates humans from other animals. A thing that we have, but they don't. Or, as Andrea thinks, maybe something that we have more of than other animals. But this is not the case. As we will see, humans do have a unique relationship to consciousness, which plays a vital role in understanding the nature of human intelligence (and its value). But consciousness is certainly not ours alone.

Consciousness is simply any form of subjective experience. Do you know that disappointing sensation of needing to pee after having just settled into bed? That's a conscious experience. So, too, is the worry that you feel knowing that you have not studied enough for an upcoming math test. Or that feeling of bittersweet sorrow as you read the final page of a book that has captured your imagination. Or even just the sound of the waves lapping at the hull of a boat, the yellowness of a banana, or the taste of stale coffee. Consciousness is what happens when your brain generates a sensation, feeling, perception, or thought of any kind that you are aware of.

To understand the tension around the question of whether animals have consciousness, we need to spend a moment drilling down into those two words that make up its definition: *subjective* and *experience*. Let's start with the concept of subjective.

If something is subjective, it means that it is being understood or experienced by someone from their perspective. In his iconic essay "What Is It Like to Be a Bat?," the philosopher Thomas Nagel argued that the subjective experience of the world as felt by an individual (human or animal) is not something that can be observed or explained in objective terms.[2] There is simply no way to get inside the head of another creature and measure their experiences. This is what philosophers call the *problem of other minds,* the inescapable fact that the subjective experience of other minds will always remain hidden inside a black box.

The word *experience* refers to the actual sensations that manifest in your mind as an emotion or thought crops up. For example, if you eat a bowl of Cheerios, it creates a flood of physical and emotional sensations that your mind experiences. These *properties of conscious experience* are what philosophers call *qualia.*[3] You can put words to your Cheerio-eating qualia, like *sugary* or *crunchy* or *disgusting* to convey to other people how you feel while eating them. Maybe if I ate the same bowl of Cheerios, I would use the same words to describe my Cheerio-eating qualia. But that doesn't mean we're describing the same conscious phenomena. It's possible that the sensations that bubble up in your mind when eating Cheerios are — if they *could* be measured objectively — entirely different from mine. But qualia are always private experiences and can't be measured objectively, so we cannot know.

Nonetheless, we're generally confident that most human beings share similar experiences of the world around us because our described qualia tend to match up. This allows me to predict quite confidently that you would prefer eating a bowl of Cheerios to a bowl of human hair. Even if my hair-eating qualia are slightly different from yours, there's a high probability that most humans experience disgust when trying to swallow a wad of hair. My confidence levels start to plummet, however, once I'm dealing with different species. Carpet beetles, for example, would love to tear into a bowl full of human hair, and probably would avoid Cheerios altogether. So, my subjective experiences of hair-eating tell me nothing about the hair-eating qualia of a carpet beetle.

The main stumbling block with attempting to guess what nonhuman animals' qualia feels like (or if they even have qualia) is that we cannot talk to them about their experiences. As we learned earlier, animals can communicate about their emotional states (like anger or fear) with signals like bared teeth or growling, but they do not have the linguistic ability to describe what these emotions feel like subjectively. So we have relied on analogies — not language — to make guesses as to what animals' qualia are like. If a chimpanzee is cradling the body of her dead infant, we can guess that she might be experiencing something analogous to human grief. After all, humans are quite closely related to chimpanzees, and this mourning behavior closely resembles our own. But this type of analogy breaks down as the animals we're thinking about get further away from us on the phylogenetic tree. For instance, what human qualia might be analogous to what an octopus experiences as she places a tentacle onto a crab and "tastes" it using the chemotactile receptors in her suckers?[4] Because octopus arms operate autonomously, this information possibly stays in her arm for processing and might never make it to her central brain. Our bodies and minds interact very differently, and so we have no real analogue to compare this to.

Despite the impossibility of measuring subjective experience and the inadequacy of human-centric analogies, many scientists and philosophers are quite confident that animals at least *have* subjective experiences. Nagel argued that being a bat feels like *something*, and I don't think I overstep by saying that many — if not most — animal cognition researchers and philosophers would agree. Which is why, in 2012, a group of them signed a document titled the Cambridge Declaration on Consciousness, which reads as follows: "Convergent evidence indicates that nonhuman animals have the neuroanatomical, neurochemical, and neurophysiological substrates of conscious states along with the capacity to exhibit intentional behaviors. Consequently, the weight of evidence indicates that humans are not unique in possessing the neurological substrates that generate consciousness. Nonhuman animals, including all mammals and birds, and many other creatures, including octopuses, also possess these neurological substrates."[5]

How are they able to argue this if subjective experience is, by definition, private and inaccessible in animals? How can they possibly *know*?

The argument for animal consciousness is based on

two lines of evidence: brains and behavior. The brain argument is relatively straightforward. We know that humans have subjective experience (i.e., consciousness). We don't know exactly *how* a brain generates consciousness, but unless you subscribe to the view that consciousness is something that happens outside of the brain, then the brain (or maybe the nervous system in general) has to be the source. Animal brains and human brains are all made of the same stuff, and in the case of mammals, brain tissue appears to be divided up in the skull along generally similar lines. Since the brain structures we suspect are involved in the subjective experience of something like fear in humans are also found in corresponding areas of the brains of most vertebrates (e.g., the insular cortex), it's reasonable to assume that they, too, experience fear subjectively.

This is a huge oversimplification, of course, but it's the thrust of the argument. In reality, scientists suspect, but don't know for sure, which structures in the human brain are responsible for the conscious experience of emotions like fear. And just because brains are structured similarly does not necessarily mean they will function identically. An MRI of my and my wife's brain would suggest that they are nearly indistinguishable structurally, and yet I will never be able to learn Old Irish grammar or sing like she can. A chimpanzee brain and the famous chef Gordon Ramsay's brain are also nearly identical when compared to the brain of a carpet beetle, and yet chimpanzees will never be able to cook a beef Wellington as well as Gordon. Analogous brain structures alone are not evidence that other animals possess analogous subjective experiences or cognitive capacities. This is why you need to pair brain structures with the behavioral evidence of animals acting as if they are conscious.

There are two types of behavioral evidence. The first is the most fun since it involves getting drunk. When humans ingest alcohol, it has a well-studied impact on the function of our minds. It can lead to the suppression of our inhibitions, lack of motor coordination, and — if you do it wrong — loss of consciousness. But we tolerate these less than desirable effects because drinking alcohol releases dopamine, which gives our brains that sensation of euphoria. In other words, we drink because it's pleasurable. Elephants, it turns out, behave the same way.

In a scientific study from the early 1980s — when giving alcohol to elephants in the name of science seemed like an acceptable thing to do — researchers presented a group of captive elephants at a safari park in California with water buckets with varying concentrations of ethanol: 0, 7, 10, 14, 25, and 50 percent.[6] The elephants were then free to drink from whichever bucket they wanted. They preferred the 7 percent alcohol solution to everything else (including plain water). After drinking the alcohol, the elephants behaved very much like drunk humans; a few stood swaying on their feet with their eyes closed. A few laid down on the ground. Most of them wrapped their trunks around themselves — something elephants do when they are feeling ill. A couple of the more aggressive elephants became even more belligerent (familiar to anyone who's witnessed a bar brawl). *In vino veritas,* which means "in wine, there is truth," applies to humans as well as elephants, it seems. This (ethically questionable) experiment shows that elephants appeared to seek out alcohol in concentrations that would make them drunk — but not too drunk — in order to experience that feeling of euphoria, which we are all too familiar with. This alcohol-seeking behavior only makes sense if two things are true: 1) alcohol affects elephant brains like it does human brains, and 2) elephants experience subjective feelings of euphoria when drinking, just like humans.

The second type of behavioral evidence involves what the Cambridge Declaration on Consciousness describes as "the capacity to exhibit intentional behaviors." Remember from Chapter 2 that an intentional behavior is one where an animal has a goal in mind, and actively monitors the situation to determine whether that goal has been achieved. This definition assumes subjective awareness of a goal; keeping something "in mind" means being conscious of one's intentions. In other words, any animal that looks like it intends to do something could be understood as displaying behavioral evidence of consciousness.

Consider the case of Bruce. He is a kea, a parrot species native to New Zealand and famous for their curiosity and problem-solving abilities. In 2013, Bruce was rescued from the wild after having lost the top half of his beak. A nonfunctional beak is a huge bummer for a kea — or any bird really. It makes eating a challenge, but also makes it much harder to engage in a behavior called *preening*. Preening is where a bird scrapes their feathers between the two halves of their beak to remove dirt and parasites. Despite his handicap, Bruce devised a solution, which resulted in one of the best arguments for the presence of intentional behavior in any animal species.[7]

When it comes time to preen, Bruce will search his enclosure for a small stone. It has to be just the right size to fit comfortably between his lower beak and his tongue. He then slides his feathers between the stone and his tongue, resulting in perfectly clean feathers. Amalia Bastos and her colleagues from the University of Auckland made an elegant case that Bruce's pebble-preening was clear evidence of intentional behavior. For starters, in 93.75 percent of cases where Bruce picked up a pebble, he used it to preen. "Bruce's manipulations of pebbles were almost always followed by preening, suggesting that he picked up the pebble with the intent of using it as a preening tool," argued Bastos. And in 95.42 percent of cases where Bruce dropped the pebble while preening, he either picked it up again or grabbed a similar pebble to continue preening. Both his ability to pinpoint the right tool and persistence in getting the job done suggest that Bruce wasn't just stumbling haphazardly into solutions to his preening problem. He had to have been intending to clean his feathers and devised a solution that was not part of a kea's normal behavioral repertoire.

"Kea do not regularly display tool use in the wild," Bastos told *The Guardian,* "so to have an individual innovate tool use in response to his disability shows great flexibility in their intelligence. They're able to adapt and flexibly solve new problems as they emerge."[8]

This is, in my opinion, a rock-solid case (pun intended) for intentional behavior in an animal. When you combine Bruce's evidence with the fact that parrots are known to get drunk on purpose (there's a tree in Australia called the Drunk Parrot Tree with fermented berries that attracts the red-collared lorikeet), and the fact that scientists have found "substantial anatomical homologies and functional similarities with mammals in the thalamocortical systems that are associated with consciousness"[9] in birds like parrots, you have a case that parrots satisfy all the criteria for having consciousness as laid out by the Cambridge Declaration on Consciousness.

It's easy to see how this line of reasoning would apply to other species that we observe engaging in innovative or flexible or intentional behavior like dolphins, elephants, and crows. Or species whose brains are structured similarly to humans like the great apes. But honeybees? Is it really the case, as I said to Andrea, that scientists think insects have the brain structures necessary to support consciousness? That they exhibit intentional behaviors like Bruce? Do insects get drunk? The answer to these questions is: yes, yes, and you betcha.

Bee brained

To help make my case, I need to introduce you to Lars Chittka. An expert on bee cognition, Chittka is a behavioral ecologist with Queen Mary University of London, and perhaps the most prominent insect intelligence evangelist around today. He has published extensively on the idea that insect brains — despite their size — have everything they need to generate complex cognition, including subjective experience. The basic argument in favor of the "who needs big brains for consciousness" stance is that, when it comes to generating complexity, it's not the number of neurons that matters, it's the way they wire together. Bee brains have just one million neurons compared to humans' eighty-five billion. But these one million neurons can create up to a billion synapses (connections to other neurons) in the bee brain, which is more than enough to create a ginormous neural network capable of massive processing power.[10] "In bigger brains we often don't find more complexity, just an endless repetition of the same neural circuits over and over," argues Chittka. "This might add detail to remembered images or sounds, but not add any degree of complexity. Bigger brains might in many cases be bigger hard drives, not necessarily better processors."[11]

What about brain structure? Surely there's something special about human (or other big-brained animals) brains in terms of *how* they wire that is what generates our consciousness? Not so, argues Chittka. "The much-sought-after neural correlate of consciousness (NCC) has not been identified in humans; thus one cannot argue that certain animals don't have human-type NCC." In other words, since we do not understand how consciousness arises from the way neurons wire and fire, we have no basis for assuming insect brains lack the necessary structures.

While science hasn't found definitive evidence for the exact neuronal structure (or combination of structures) that generate subjective experience, we do know that insect brains have brain structures that we *suspect* are correlated with consciousness in animals. For insects, there's a structure called a *central complex* that generates cognitive processes we associate with consciousness. It's a place in their brain that integrates information from the senses, which in turns helps an insect navigate their environment by creating a mental model of themselves and the world around them. According to the philosopher Colin Klein and the neurobiologist Andrew Barron, because mammals have analogous structures in their midbrains that appear to do these same things, and because these structures and cognitive skills are generally understood to be involved in consciousness for humans, there is "strong evidence that the insect brain has the capacity to support subjective experience."[12] All this to say that, while we can't say for certain that insects have the brain parts needed to generate consciousness, there is a perfectly good argument to be made that they do.

What about insect behavior, though? Are their tiny brains generating complex behavior that suggests consciousness? It appears so. Consider this famous experiment conducted by Chittka and his team on bumblebees. To test their ability for complex learning, the bees were given a food-reward task unlike anything they might encounter in nature. A tiny plastic ball was placed in a dish that had a target drawn at the center of it. If the bees could grab and drag the ball to the target, they would receive a sugar-water reward. Bumblebee foraging behavior in the wild does not require a skill of this sort, yet they were able to do it. A remarkable feat on its own, but not as remarkable as what happened next. In a follow-up experiment, three balls were placed at different distances from the center of the dish.[13] The two balls closest to the center were glued down, so to nail the task, the bumblebee learned that she needed to move the farthest one. Meanwhile, an observer bee that was unfamiliar with the experiment had been watching these "demonstrator" bees solve the task from outside the testing area. When the observer bee was then allowed to enter the testing area for the first time, she did something that revealed that she truly understood the nature of the task at hand. This time, the balls were no longer glued down. Instead of simply copying what she has seen the other bee do (i.e., grab the farthest ball), she made a beeline to the closest ball and dragged it to the target. She was not just imitating the behavior of the other bee through associative learning. She knew that a ball had to go on the target and that it made the most sense to grab the closest ball. She had thought about the problem and devised a better strategy. Chittka argued that this demonstrates that bees have "a basic understanding of the outcome of their own actions, and those of other bees: that is, consciousness-like phenomena or intentionality."[14] If that's the case, then this is evidence that bees satisfy the intentional behavior criterion as outlined in the Cambridge Declaration on Consciousness.

And lastly, there is evidence that insects seek out mind-altering substances. Consider this unusual but elegant study from the neuroscientist Galit Shohat-Ophir.[15] Her team bred fruit flies with brains that would generate a specific neuropeptide — corazonin — whenever they were exposed to a red light. Corazonin usually floods the brain whenever a male fruit fly ejaculates, so switching on a red light should induce an affective (emotional) state similar to an orgasm. Unsurprisingly, the researchers found that these altered flies clearly preferred spending time in the areas of their enclosure illuminated by red light. As part of the experiment, one group of male fruit flies were exposed to a lot of red light over the course of a few days, while another group didn't have the orgasm-inducing red light turned on a single time. When given the choice of two foods to consume, the flies that had been deprived of the red light — and thus not orgasming for three days straight — ate more of the food containing ethanol. In other words, they got themselves drunk. Meanwhile, the flies that had been enjoying a steady stream of red light–induced pleasure didn't really want the alcohol-laced food. The fact that the orgasm-deprived fruit flies opted for mind-altering drugs — presumably in search of an endorphin rush — suggests that they had some awareness of their own decreased happiness levels and intentionally turned to alcohol to make themselves feel better. As Lars Chittka stated in response to this study: "Why would an organism seek out mind-altering substances when there isn't a mind to alter?"[16]

All this evidence points to the very real possibility that subjective experience — consciousness — is something that insects have. If that's so, consciousness is a trait that must have evolved very early on in our evolutionary history from an ancient common ancestor of humans and flies, which is likely an ocean-dwelling invertebrate that lived five hundred million years ago.[17] Which means, by my definition, that most animals alive today probably have consciousness. If that's the case, then why is it that your average Joe (or your average Andrea in my case) thinks it's so absurd that insects (or chickens) might be conscious? That, as Andrea put it, they just run on instinct like little robots? There is a long history of thinking of animals this way, going back to the seventeenth-century philosopher René Descartes, who labeled nonhuman animals *bête machine:* animal/beast machines. In other words, Andrea's in perfectly good company. And I dare say that many animal cognition folks are still skeptical of the claim that insects have subjective experience, although I am personally on team Chittka.

The reason for the skepticism is quite simple. When most people use the word *consciousness,* they are not talking solely about subjective experience. They include other cognitive traits, like self-awareness. Andrea had said that it was crazy to assume my honeybee drones were conscious specifically because she thought it was impossible that they were self-aware. But self-awareness and consciousness are not synonymous. People also include cognitive skills like episodic foresight or even theory of mind when they think about consciousness. In fact, there are a ton of cognitive traits that we conflate with consciousness. I will explain more about these differences later in the chapter, which will help us develop a more nuanced understanding of the value placed on human consciousness. But before I do, we need to understand a bit more about how consciousness works in tandem with all these other processes to generate the human and animal mind in the first place.

Improv on the brain

There are many models for describing the nature of consciousness as it relates to cognition and neurobiology, but it's not an easy subject to wrap your head around. I have found the best way to make sense of something this complex is to relate it to something I already know about. In this case, improv. Improv — or improvisational theater — is a form of unscripted theater spontaneously generated by a group of improvisers on stage. Aside from being a fantastic way to get your creative juices flowing and share some belly laughs with friends, it's also the perfect metaphor for how minds work.

Think of your mind as a theater that is putting on an improv show.[18] There is a stage, dimly lit except for a spotlight. On the stage are a dozen or so improvisers, all of whom are champing at the bit for their chance to stand in the spotlight. In this metaphor, the spotlight is equivalent to subjective experience (i.e., consciousness). Whatever the improviser standing in that spotlight is doing is transformed into qualia that the rest of your mind experiences. These qualia flood over the other improvisers on stage, the audience, and everyone working behind the scenes: the sound people in the booth, the director standing in the balcony, the stage managers hiding in the wings, etc. Everyone is watching what happens in that spotlight. Thus, the contents of conscious experience are broadcast across the mind, and available to a huge number of cognitive processes for analysis.

In this metaphor, the people onstage are all things that you *could* be conscious of. This includes sensory input from the things you see, hear, or touch. But also, internal motivational states like hunger, or emotional states like fear. The people offstage are all *subconscious* processes which never produce qualia of their own, but are nonetheless vital to the improv performance (i.e., the operation of your mind). Maybe the assistant stage manager is like muscle memory: your ability to, for example, ride a bicycle. Once learned, bike riding is something an unconscious part of your brain takes care of automatically. If a stage manager is doing their job correctly, they are never seen, operating at the level of the subconscious. And yet, without a stage manager, the improv show couldn't exist.

The theater of your mind is populated primarily by unconscious things that will never stand in that spotlight. Like the part of your mind that controls your heartbeat and digestive system. Or the unconscious biases and heuristics that our minds use to make quick decisions. Daniel Kahneman described these as the System 1 mode of thinking in his book *Thinking, Fast and Slow*: instant, automatic decisions made by subconscious cognitive processes operating behind the scenes.

Importantly, you can't have an improv show without someone in the spotlight. System 1 thinking can't put on a show all by itself. The reason minds (including animal minds) have this spotlight — the reason they have consciousness — is to help an animal make everyday decisions that require a bit of deliberation. The spotlight is there to tell the rest of your mind who the star of the show is at that moment, and everyone chips in to help that improviser move the show forward. In other words, consciousness exists to help your mind make decisions and generate behavior.

Like on an actual improv stage, the improvisers who end up attracting the spotlight are the ones who do something novel or unexpected, or who demand attention by making a lot of noise. By being the focus of attention, the loudest improviser can recruit multiple cognitive systems — including the unconscious ones watching the improv show — to help solve a problem or decide on what to do next.

Here's an example. Let's say that you are sitting on the couch reading a book. This behavior activates several cognitive systems, including your comprehension and linguistics abilities, which are largely unconscious. The spotlight is focusing on the imagined visual images evoked by the words on the page, generating qualia that the rest of your mind is currently enjoying. Suddenly, a new improviser jumps into the spotlight: hunger. The theater of your mind is now focused on the hunger qualia being shouted from the stage. This hunger improviser causes a cascade of action in a huge number of cognitive systems in your mind. Some subconscious system responsible for your motor action begins closing your book — it's now time to search for a snack. Maybe you have a sudden craving for a Snickers bar — perhaps an unconscious response to a Snickers advertisement that you saw last night on TV. This is the equivalent to an audience member shouting "Snickers!," which the improvisers must react to. A stage manager will whisper to the performer that they remember seeing a Snickers in the kitchen. This stage manager represents your unconscious memory system. Now another improviser pops into the spotlight for a second: episodic foresight. They've come onstage to provide backup to help move the scene along. Episodic foresight generates the conscious experience of you looking through your snack drawer in the kitchen, where the stage manager said the Snickers was located. This combination of cognitive systems — both on- and offstage — now leads to your decision to walk into the kitchen to look for a Snickers bar.

Whenever an animal must make a decision where a bit of thinking and deliberation are required, the spotlight of subjective experience needs to make an appearance so that qualia can be generated. Qualia are the currency of action. Or, as the philosopher Susanne Langer wrote, "to feel is to do something."[19] This is the reason animals evolved subjective experience in the first place, and why it makes the most sense to think of consciousness as a vital part of any animal's mind.

More conscious is not a thing

I hope you're still with me at this point, Andrea, because now is the time when I can reveal the reason why human consciousness seems so different from that of animals'. This improv show model has exposed something important. Human consciousness *is* in fact special for this reason:

We, as a species, have a much larger number of cognitive processes that are potentially able to step into the spotlight of consciousness and generate qualia for us. We're not more conscious, we're just conscious of more things. This is an important difference to understand, so I will provide an example from my life to illustrate the point.

A few years ago, my friend Monica was explaining the concept of aphantasia, a disorder that she had. This is the inability for some people (approximately 1 percent of the population) to see images in their mind's eye. "When people with aphantasia close their eyes, they see only blackness, never able to conjure up the image of, say, an apple," she explained.

"That's sad. So, wait a minute — if you close your eyes, you're unable to think of an apple?" I asked.

"No. That's not it. I can think of an apple, I just can't see it as if it were a photograph. Like normal people can."

"Right," I said. "But, of course, nobody can actually see an image of an apple in their mind's eye as if it were a photograph. That's crazy."

"Most people can."

"But that's impossible. I mean, when I close my eyes, I know that I am thinking of what an apple looks like. I just don't see an apple."

"Umm, Justin? I think you might have aphantasia, too."

I asked my wife if, when she closed her eyes and tried to picture an apple, she actually "saw" a picture of an apple. She said she could. Everyone else I asked confirmed that they can see photograph-like images of apples in their mind's eye, with varying levels of detail and intensity. But I see nothing. Monica was right. It turns out that I, too, have aphantasia.

Unlike a neurotypical human, my conscious mind is incapable of generating imagined images of things to help it figure out, for example, where in the supermarket the peanut butter is located. The thing is, I know the peanut butter's location in the store and I can describe where it is using words. I can "feel" its location somehow. I just can't "see" the layout of the store in my mind. I lack a capacity for conscious visual imagination. When I read a science fiction book, I cannot conjure images of the space stations that are being described. I cannot close my eyes and see my daughter's face. And yet, I guarantee that I am no less conscious than other human beings. My experience of consciousness as it flits across that improv stage feels the same as yours. I just have one fewer improviser waiting to step into the spotlight.

The players on the human stage

When we think about animal consciousness, what we really want to know is not if they have it (because they do), or how much consciousness they have (the same amount), but which cognitive processes each species is able to send out onto that improv stage. When I say that humans are conscious of more things, what does that mean exactly? It means that human minds evolved to allow us to be consciously aware of a large number of cognitive processes that are either completely unique to our species, or things that, for most animals, only happen on the subconscious level. To see what I mean, let's first consider the kinds of things that most animals would have available to that spotlight of subjective experience: emotions and feelings.

The word *emotion* comes from the Latin word *emovere,* which means to move out or agitate. This etymological fact helps us understand that emotions are states of activation in the brain whose goal is to *agitate* an animal into *moving out* and doing things that will ensure its survival.[20] The neurobiologist Jaak Panksepp coined the term *affective neuroscience* to describe the study of the underlying neurology that generates emotional states in the animal (and human) mind, and identified seven classes of emotions that you're likely to find in most mammals: *seeking, lust, care, play, rage, fear,* and *panic.*[21] Much of animal behavior can be explained by the way these seven affective systems interact with our mind to motivate us to do things that help us live long enough to sire offspring. Seeking makes us want to find food and shelter. Lust makes us want to mate. Care helps us nurture our offspring or aid our social partners. Play helps us maintain those social partners while also honing our physical skills. Rage makes us defend ourselves, our food resources, and our homes from attackers. Fear tells us which things to avoid or defend against. And panic gives us a reason to seek out social partners in the first place.

Many of these emotions likely exist in similar forms in the minds of non-mammalian species as well. And many of these subconscious emotions will likely get translated into conscious experiences so animals will be better equipped to make decisions. When subconscious emotions make their way onto that improv stage and into the spotlight of subjective awareness for use in decision-making, scientists sometimes give them a new name: *feelings*. Frans de Waal elegantly explains in his book *Mama's Last Hug* that feelings "happen when emotions bubble to the surface so that we become aware of them."[22]

Humans, however, are unique: We have many more emotions that get translated into conscious feelings. Like that feeling of fairness we saw in the study of macaques, which likely exists for primates, but maybe not honeybees. Or things like nostalgia, that rely on our unique capacity for mental time travel. Or guilt, which relies on the unique way we relate to others via theory of mind. Unfortunately, because of the *problem of other minds*, it is notoriously difficult to tell just by observing animal behavior whether it is experiencing complex or basic feelings. For example, on the first day of class for my Animal Minds course, I show students a YouTube video of Denver the dog.[23] While his owner was out of the house, Denver ate a bag of cat treats. With the camera rolling, the owner asks Denver if he was the one that ate the treats. Denver avoids eye contact. He droops his ears, squints, and licks his chops — looking every bit like he's experiencing guilt at having eaten the cat's treats. When I ask the students what's happening in Denver's mind at that moment, they all reach the commonsense conclusion that Denver feels guilty. I then go on to show research into what submissive body language looks like in dogs, and how Denver's behavior can be elicited from any dog when in the presence of a confrontational owner regardless of whether they did something wrong. That's not to say that a dog couldn't be consciously aware of violating some sort of norm leading to guilt. It's just that the behaviors displayed by Denver occur whenever a dog is trying to avoid a fight with another dog or human. In other words, it is more likely to be the behavioral expression of one of Panksepp's more basic affective states: *fear.*

Aside from emotions, animal brains generate homeostatic sensations like hunger or thirst. Given how vital these are to agitating us into action, it is likely that they, too, are experienced subjectively by animals. And then, of course, there are sensory affects, including pain, temperature, pressure, or really anything that our sense organs (eyes, ears, skin, tongue, etc.) send to our brains. All these basic sensory signals are used by the nonconscious parts of our mind to generate automatic, System 1–style behavior (e.g., pulling your hand away when you touch a burning hot cookie sheet). But sensory signals often make their way into conscious awareness as well. This helps us plan our more complicated behavior, like looking for an oven mitt to put on our hand so we don't burn ourselves on the cookie sheet again. Panksepp argued that all mammal brains (and perhaps some other species as the Cambridge Declaration on Consciousness argues) have subcortical regions capable of producing these emotional, homeostatic, and sensory affective states.

The beautiful thing about the affective systems of nonhuman animals is that each species will have a tapestry of sensations available to it that are unique to its sensory, physiological, or social systems. Dolphins, for example, can channel bizarre perceptual information to their conscious mind via their ability to echolocate. By sending click sounds out into the water, dolphins can create acoustic images detailing the shape, density, and movement of objects in their environment. Echolocation can even penetrate some substances, allowing them to "see" fish buried in the sand using sound. Dolphins can also eavesdrop on the echolocation signals of other dolphins swimming next to them. This gives dolphins an ability to know — on a level that's beyond human comprehension — precisely what their friends are perceiving. It would be a bit like me getting an image in my mind of what you were seeing on your smartphone just by sitting next to you on the couch with my eyes closed. This is a cognitive and conscious process wholly foreign to a human, but it plays a major role in how dolphins go about their lives. The animal kingdom is absolutely flooded with animal cognitive, affective, and sensory processes for which there is no analogue in humans. It doesn't make these animal species "more conscious" than us. It just gives each species' improv stage a different set of improvisers to work with.

Which brings us to humans. Aside from having a few complex emotions/feelings that other animals might lack, humans are unique because of the sheer number of things available to our conscious minds, as well as the complexity of those things. Let's start with this idea of self-awareness.

There is no such thing as a singular concept of self-awareness. This term encompasses many "awarenesses," which different species possess in different forms. There are three main categories: temporal self-awareness, body self-awareness, and social self-awareness.[24] Importantly, an animal can possess one of these types of self-awareness without it being available to consciousness. That might sound weird, but here's how it works.

For example, temporal self-awareness is the mind's capacity to understand that it will continue to exist in the (near) future. Pretty much all minds must have this baked in. Otherwise, animals would never be able to have goals or intentions. Bruce the parrot, for example, intended to preen his feathers with the help of a stone. The only possible way his mind could coordinate this behavior is if his mind was aware that it would continue to exist in the future. But that doesn't mean that Bruce's temporal self-awareness was standing on that improv stage, receiving the spotlight of consciousness. For humans, we know what happens when we are aware of our temporal self-awareness: We can engage in mental time travel and episodic foresight. When temporal self-awareness is onstage, we can take that feeling of "my mind exists and will continue to exist" and broadcast it to all the other cognitive systems. Doing so allows us to imagine our mind existing in the past, future, and eventually existing no more (i.e., death wisdom). But since it does not appear that Bruce (or many other animals) can envision themselves in similar circumstances, we can only assume that temporal self-awareness never steps onto the stage for him. And yet, he can still engage in goal-directed behavior because his temporal self-awareness provides the unconscious scaffolding upon which his mind rests.

The same is true for body self-awareness. This is the awareness of one's own body as being a thing that exists in the world and is separate from other things, and that can be controlled by the mind. The fact that any animal appears to be able to move its body through space and interact with objects suggests that body self-awareness is a rather basic kind of cognitive skill. One of the classic tests of self-awareness in animals has been the mirror self-recognition test (MSR). This involves putting a mark on the body or head of an animal without them noticing and then giving them access to a mirror. If they use the mirror to inspect the weird new mark that they see on themselves, we could assume that they know that it's themselves they see in the mirror and are thus "self-aware." Many species "pass" this test, including chimpanzees, dolphins, elephants, etc. But what this test might actually reveal is the fact that, for some species, their body self-awareness is available for conscious consideration. For those species that fail the MSR test, like dogs or cats, it would be ridiculous to suggest that they are not aware of their bodies. Their mind is busy controlling that body all day long, so it must have some concept of body self-awareness tucked away in there. But it's entirely possible that dogs and cats are not able to *consciously* consider the nature of their body like a chimpanzee can, which is why cats and dogs are flummoxed by mirrors.

Lastly, we have social self-awareness. This is the ability to be consciously aware of your relationship to others in your social world when it comes to social status or the strength or nature of your relationships. It gives us the ability to see ourselves as others might see us, allowing for theory of mind to take root. It also gives us the ability to lie (and bullshit), as well as make predictions about how others behave based on what we think others know or believe. And it gives us the ability to analyze our behavior in relation to that of others, which helps transform our norms into morals. As we have seen for animals, many have social self-awareness. For example, it drives the formation of the pecking order for my chickens. But it's unlikely that my chickens are — or would need to be — consciously aware of their social selves. Chicken society runs perfectly fine being regulated by unconscious norms without them needing to consciously ruminate on their status within the flock. But conscious rumination of the social self for humans leads to the kind of amazing social complexity we see in human culture, as well as complex moral, ethical, and legal systems we can create (for whatever that's worth).

When we ask questions about animal intelligence, we are very often wondering about the extent to which other species could thrust these three kinds of awarenesses onto the stage of consciousness. It's an interesting question, since having the ability to think about yourself (individually or as part of a group) greatly increases one's ability to generate complex behavior. Humans might well be unique because of our ability to have all three forms of self-awareness available for conscious analysis.

Add to that the ability to be conscious of your own thinking/cognition. This is called *metacognition*. To understand this concept, I will give you my favorite example. Researchers at the Dolphin Research Center in Florida trained a dolphin named Natua to press one paddle when he heard a high tone (2,100 Hz) and a different paddle when he heard a low tone (anything below 2,100 Hz). Natua would get a fish reward for pressing the correct paddle, or a long time-out for pressing the wrong one. A time-out would mean that the experiment would stop for a while, which means no chance for Natua to receive a fish reward. It was a rather simple task for Natua until the low tone was so close to the high tone that he could no longer discriminate between the two. At that point, he just started randomly pressing paddles. This was no fun for Natua, since a wrong answer would mean no fish for a while.

To see if Natua was aware of his uncertainty when the tones became difficult to distinguish, a third paddle was introduced: the bailout paddle. If Natua pressed the bailout paddle, he would just have to wait for a bit until a new, easy-to-discriminate tone was presented and he could try again. This was the best option in those cases where he was unsure if the tone was low or high, where getting it wrong meant a long wait.

When presented with a low tone that was difficult for him to differentiate from the high tone, Natua reacted exactly as you would expect of an animal that was having a hard time figuring out the answer. He would slowly approach the paddles and sweep his head from side to side — clearly hesitating — before eventually pressing the bailout paddle. The best explanation for this behavior was that Natua knew (via metacognition) that he didn't know the right answer, and was consciously aware of the difficulty he was having in solving the problem. In other words, Natua's thought processes were standing on the stage in the full spotlight of conscious awareness, allowing him to think about his thinking.

Metacognition gives an animal the ability to be aware of when it doesn't know something. To think about its own knowledge. Being aware of one's ignorance drives the search for more knowledge to help in the decision-making process. There are only a handful of studies (and a lot of controversy) suggesting that a few animal species have metacognition along these lines, including research with monkeys, dolphins, apes, dogs, and rats. If metacognition exists in animals (as it certainly appears to for Natua), it might not be particularly widespread. In contrast, this ability is the bedrock of human thinking. We clearly have conscious awareness of our metacognition, which inspires us to pinpoint gaps and problems in our thinking and seek out solutions using all the other cognitive abilities at our disposal. We use math and language to consciously organize our thoughts, and thanks to our capacity for causal inference and episodic foresight, we can imagine infinite solutions to the problems we face.

The explanation for a human's ability to do complex stuff we are keen to label "intelligent" is in fact related to our capacity for consciousness. But only in the sense that we have an array of cognitive processes in our minds upon which we can train our spotlight of subjective experience allowing us to coordinate these cognitive processes more efficiently to solve complex problems. All animals are living qualia-rich lives, regardless of the complexity or number of cognitive processes they have available to them that could stand on that improv stage and be illuminated by the spotlight of conscious, subjective experience.

So I am convinced, my dear friend Andrea, that I was in fact making the lives of those doomed drones a little bit happier. I suspect that their little minds were conscious of the pleasure of eating honey that one last time before they died. And yet, there is no doubt that the human mind is conscious of much more than the mind of those drones. You are right that there is something different about the contents of our consciousness, as we've seen. The question is: So what? Is everything that we've accomplished as a species because of these cognitive abilities — and our subjective awareness of them — either 1) a sign that our species is successful, and 2) a good thing for the planet? Those are the big questions that we'll tackle next.

Chapter 6

Prognostic Myopia

Our shortsighted farsightedness

> The press, the machine, the railway, the telegraph are premises whose thousand-year conclusion no one has yet dared to draw.
>
> — Nietzsche[1]

Capability Brown was England's most celebrated gardener. He's also a teensy bit responsible for the impending extinction of the human species.

Born Lancelot Brown in 1715, he was given "Capability" as a nickname; it was a word he used often when explaining to English aristocrats that their estates had "great capability for improvement."[2] He preferred a naturalistic look to his gardens: replacing the heavily manicured hedges, stone pathways, and grand fountains typical of seventeenth-century formal French gardens with grand vistas overlooking lakes, groves of statuesque trees, and sprawling lawns. He upgraded the gardens of 170 British estates in his day, including Highclere Castle, which has become famous as the exterior location for the historical drama *Downton Abbey*. The opening credits depict a man and his dog walking over a perfectly manicured lawn — originally designed by Capability — with the castle looming in the background. Capability's dangerous legacy is shaped by precisely this kind of lawn.

Notably, George Washington and Thomas Jefferson were huge fans of his work. Both Jefferson's Monticello estate and Washington's Mount Vernon estate were modeled to resemble a Capability design and are considered some of the most famous gardens in the United States. They were portrayed on countless postcards strewn across the kitchen tables of millions of American homes by the early nineteenth century. These iconic houses had sprawling lawns where, if the postcards were to be believed, well-heeled sophisticates would stroll about with parasols playing badminton. Lawns were part of a burgeoning aesthetic ethos suggesting that the American experiment would yield domestic prosperity — and plenty of free time to smack shuttlecocks about — for all those who wished to work hard and make something of themselves. It was a dream that applied to everyone except, of course, the enslaved people who were forced to trim and maintain those lawns, which is the kind of paradox the country reckons with to this day.

In the early nineteenth century, the average American

didn't have the time, money, or enslaved labor necessary to cultivate a lawn. Only the ultra-rich could afford such luxuries. With the invention of the lawn mower in 1830 by Edwin Beard Budding, however, the lawn became far more accessible. Over the course of the next century, they grew to become symbols of personal — and national — prosperity. As the car became the dominant mode of transportation in America, the front garden became an opportunity to display one's success, letting motorists *ooh* and *ahh* as they rode down suburban streets. A close-cropped front lawn tucked behind a white picket fence soon became — and remains to this day — the ultimate symbol of Americana.

Americans *love* their lawns. There are 163,812 square kilometers (about forty million acres) of domestic lawns in the United States right now.[3] That's equivalent to the size of the state of Florida. Twenty percent of Massachusetts, Rhode Island, Delaware, and Connecticut are covered by lawns.[4] A whopping 75 percent of the 116 million households in the US have a lawn of some kind.[5] Setting aside all the other ways in which our species has transformed the land on this planet, our obsession with creating lawns has altered the landscape in ways that have no equivalent in the animal kingdom. The closest you'll get is the vast network of ancient termite mounds in eastern Brazil. These huge mounds (typically eight feet tall) crisscross an area of Brazil totaling 230,000 square kilometers, and can be seen from space.[6] They are built more or less every twenty meters, and there are two hundred million of them. The termites began building these mounds almost four thousand years ago. They formed slowly as termites came to the surface to toss out the unwanted dirt from the network of tunnels excavated for transportation and their living quarters. They are, essentially, majestic garbage dumps. But, unlike human lawns, these mounds create a positive impact on the environment, forming the bottom layer of the Brazilian caatinga: a desert forest teeming with biodiversity and home to 187 species of bees, 516 birds, and 148 mammals, not to mention more than a thousand plant species.[7]

I've probably spent a thousand hours cutting grass for personal or professional reasons over the course of my life. And, frankly, I feel hoodwinked by Capability Brown and the Founding Fathers. Lawns are a monoculture wasteland that are almost entirely useless as a habitat for wildlife. They don't provide us with any food, but nonetheless require a huge investment in time, money, and resources. They are a love letter to *conspicuous consumption,* a term coined by economist Thorstein Veblen in his book The *Theory of the Leisure Class,* and defined as "the purchase of goods or services for the specific purpose of displaying one's wealth."[8] Lawns are also a giant middle finger to the environmental movement. Americans use nine billion gallons of water a day on lawns alone — that's about one-third of all domestic water usage.[9] About half of that is wasted, never reaching the roots due to evaporation, wind, and runoff. Add to that the 1.2 billion gallons of gasoline used in lawn-mowers each year, which is even worse for the environment than it sounds. Since lawn mower engines are nowhere near as efficient as, say, those found in cars, they end up using more gasoline and creating more CO_2. Put another way, using a gas-powered mower for one hour is the equivalent of driving a hundred miles in a car.[10] The Environmental Protection Agency estimates that lawn maintenance accounts for 4 percent of annual total CO_2 emissions in the US.[11] That's a crap ton of carbon dioxide dumped into the atmosphere each year in pursuit of — well, what exactly?

Of course, it's not really Capability's fault, right? He couldn't have predicted where his horticultural endeavors would lead. Nonetheless, let's assume a hypothetical. If a time traveler from today were to go back to the eighteenth century, sit Capability down, and explain how his lawn idea would evolve into a cultural obsession that would contribute to climate change and threaten the existence of the human species, would he have shelved the idea? I doubt it. Humans have an amazing ability to justify our actions even if there is evidence that there will be negative consequences in the future. Even the most charismatic and persuasive time traveler would have a hard time convincing Capability to give up his life's work. Consider it this way: We now know the dangers of burning fossil fuels, and yet our lawn obsession continues. Threats of a postapocalyptic Earth will not stop us from maintaining our lawns, even if we understand the risks associated with this nonsensical yet wide-spread habit.

This brand of cognitive dissonance is what I call *prognostic myopia*. Prognostic myopia is the human capacity to think about and alter the future coupled with an inability to actually care all that much about what happens in the future. It's caused by the human ability to make complex decisions availing of our unique cognitive skills that result in long-term consequences. But because our minds evolved primarily to deal with immediate — not future — outcomes, we rarely experience or even understand the consequences of these long-term decisions. It is the most dangerous flaw in human thinking. So dangerous that it might lead to the extinction of our species. Which is why I will dedicate a whole chapter to explaining what prognostic myopia is, how it came into existence, how it affects our everyday lives, and why it's an extinction-level threat to humanity.

What is prognostic myopia?

Like all animals, humans live in a world where we must make decisions on a day-to-day basis that satisfy our day-to-day needs: food, shelter, sex, etc. This kind of in-the-moment decision-making is as old as life itself and fundamental to biology. But the human capacity for causal reasoning, episodic foresight, conscious deliberation, etc. gives us the ability to enact solutions to these daily now-problems with future consequences on a scale that has never been seen in the history of life on this planet. We can invent solutions that rely on technology and engineering whose, as Nietzsche wrote, "thousand-year conclusion no one has yet dared to draw." Like all animals, our biology compels us to deal with the here and now, but unlike other animals, our decisions can generate technologies that will have harmful impacts on the world for generations to come. This disconnect is at the heart of prognostic myopia.

Here's an example. Let's say you wanted to grab a snack right now. Ten thousand years ago, you might've walked a few feet into the forest, stuck your hand into a log, and yanked out a handful of tasty termites. Boom. Problem solved. Snack acquired. These days, you might walk a few feet into the kitchen and grab a banana. Same problem (hunger), same solution (food).

The difference between the two is that the availability of the banana today is shaped entirely by human-made, technological processes that have added unimaginable complexity to the simple act of grabbing a snack. And these processes generate long-term consequences we hadn't considered. What do I mean by these human-made processes?

If you're like me, you live in a part of the world where bananas do not grow naturally. Most bananas — the ones sold by Dole, Del Monte, Chiquita, etc. — are grown on plantations in South America. Which means that these bananas will need to be trucked to the nearest South American port, loaded onto a plane or a boat, and sent halfway around the world, processed domestically, distributed in grocery stores, and then, because you purchased it, land in your fruit bowl. If you shop in a supermarket with ludicrous packaging policies, you might have to first unwrap your banana from a plastic bag. You will then marvel at its color and shape, two factors engineered by a cocktail of fertilizers and pesticides used to grow them. Obviously, there is an intense carbon footprint associated with shipping bananas around the world and stuffing them into bags made from petroleum products. Not to mention the environmental impacts of pesticide- and fertilizer-based monoculture on lands (usually ancient rain forests) that have been cleared of native vegetation to support our banana cravings. The point is, our hankering for a snack in the twenty-first century is identical to what it was ten thousand years ago, but our complex cognition allows us to engage in activities (e.g., oil and gas extraction, mechanized farming, soil depletion) on a massive scale, which is transforming this planet into an uninhabitable shithole. Our kitchens are full of foods that come from a global agricultural-industrial complex that is fundamentally problematic to the survival of the human species.

This banana example highlights the two major negative consequences of prognostic myopia. The first is that humans, unlike other animals, can create long-term solutions to our problems that will have unforeseen consequences on future generations. Like the clearing of rain forests so we can satisfy our urge for a banana, or the depletion of our water reserves so we can grow our Capability Brown–inspired lawns. The second is that even in those cases where we can foresee negative consequences of our long-term solutions, our minds are not wired to truly care about those consequences in the way we would if the consequences were more immediate. You're not wired to care about the future impacts of clearing Brazilian rain forests for banana monoculture. You're wired to pick up that banana at the grocery store and throw it in your cart. This kind of indifference is exactly why a time traveler could never convince Capability Brown to un-invent lawns.

To understand how prognostic myopia came into being, we need to first understand why animal decision-making is so bad at dealing with future problems.

Humans can't feel the future

We learned in the previous chapter how subjective experience (i.e., consciousness) allows our brains to recruit multiple cognitive systems to help make complex decisions. Humans have several unique cognitive abilities that can step out onto that improv stage and receive the spotlight of subjective awareness when we are making decisions, including causal inference, mental time travel, episodic foresight, and temporal self-awareness. But there is a plethora of *unconscious* cognitive systems that also contribute. These two systems — the conscious and unconscious — work in tandem to generate our decision-making behavior. And ultimately lead to prognostic myopia. To understand how this works, let's start with a discussion of my favorite animal in the world: my daughter.

My daughter, like many school-aged kids, is grumpy in the mornings. She can get a bit snippy, and is prone to bleak tweeny pronouncements, like "I hate school and everyone and everything." It's not much fun for anyone. Here's a pro parenting tip: Telling your tween to "stop being so negative" is pointless. Instead, why not try an old-school behavioral manipulation technique: operant conditioning. It's such a powerful means of unconsciously modifying behavior that you can use it on your child even if they are fully aware that they're being manipulated.

With the goal of getting my daughter to be nicer in the mornings, I sat her down and explained how my operant conditioning plan for her was going to work (and what operant conditioning was). The basic idea is that she would get an immediate, positive reward every time she produced a desired behavior. In our case, she would receive one piece of cheese popcorn every time she said something nice. Soon, her brain would make an indelible association between saying nice things and getting a yummy treat. Her subconscious mind would then prompt her to generate positive statements to get the endorphin hit that comes with popcorn consumption. This is exactly how a scientist might approach an animal behavior experiment, but in this case, I could tell my animal subject exactly what was in store for her. We both accepted that what we were doing was trying to train her brain to generate more happiness, a goal she was fully on board with.

And it worked like gangbusters.

Each morning, I would fill a Ziploc bag with cheese popcorn and carry it around with me, tossing her a piece whenever she said things like "It's cold out this morning, but at least I have a warm jacket." Or, "I'm looking forward to eating macaroni and cheese for lunch today." Our mornings were suddenly brighter and happier, and everyone's mood improved. She wasn't necessarily happy to go to school, but she was happier than she was before.

This is one of the oldest methods that brains have for generating decisions. From fruit flies to tweens, brains learn quickly that generating certain behaviors will result in immediate positive (or negative) consequences. It's a simple, ancient decision-making hack that generates a kind of heuristic. In psychology, a heuristic is a mental shortcut or rule of thumb, often unconscious, that helps us make quick decisions. My daughter no longer needed to waste time thinking about the half a dozen possible things she could say around the breakfast table, and micro-analyze the extent to which each remark would annoy her parents. Instead, operant conditioning shoved her brain down the path of pleasantness.

Obviously, a brain that is making snap decisions is one that is not considering long-term consequences. Subconscious, snap decision-making, then, is integral to the problem of prognostic myopia. To appreciate its role, we need to appreciate just how commonplace these subconscious heuristics are in human decision-making.

If you've walked through an airport bookstore in the past twenty years, chances are you've stumbled across any number of popular science books chock-full of examples of ways in which human decision-making is governed — if not dominated — by unconscious processes. Like *Blink* by Malcom Gladwell, which argues that the decisions we make automatically (i.e., without conscious thought) are often better than ones we spend hours or days pondering. Or *Thinking, Fast and Slow* by Daniel Kahneman, which shows just how often we rely on our fast/automatic/unconscious thinking to make decisions (i.e., System 1), vs. our slow/calculating/conscious thinking (i.e., System 2). He describes them as follows: "Systems 1 and 2 are both active whenever we are awake. System 1 runs automatically and System 2 is normally in comfortable low-effort mode, in which only a fraction of its capacity is engaged. System 1 continuously generates suggestions for System 2: impressions, intuitions, intentions, and feelings. If endorsed by System 2, impressions and intuitions turn into beliefs, and impulses turn into voluntary actions. When all goes smoothly, which is most of the time, System 2 adopts the suggestions of System 1 with little or no modification."[12]

Many influential books expound on the idea of the power and prevalence of unconscious thought, including *Nudge* by Richard H. Thaler, *The Power of Habit* by Charles Duhigg, *How We Decide* by Jonah Lehrer, *Sway* by Ori Brafman, and *Why Choose This Book?* by Read Montague. Among them is Dan Ariely, author of *Predictably Irrational.* Ariely is a behavioral economist who studies human decision-making and has helped popularize the idea that humans are not the kind of rational, conscious decision-makers that we'd like to think we are. He argues that we are pushed — unconsciously — into making decisions by the structure of the environment around us. It's the external environment that triggers heuristics and cognitive biases that generate our behavior without any need for conscious rumination or rationality. An example he often cites is organ donor behavior.[13] A now famous study by Eric Johnson and Daniel Goldstein found that some European countries had extremely high rates of people who consented to donating their organs after death, while some had very low rates.[14] These consent rates didn't seem to have anything to do with cultural differences. Countries like the Netherlands had a donation consent rate of 27.5 percent, whereas Belgium, their immediate neighbor, and with whom they share close cultural and linguistic ties, had a consent rate of 98 percent. The significant difference had nothing to do with the way that either felt about organ donation or end-of-life decisions. Instead, it had to do with the organ donation form they were being asked to fill out when applying for a license.

The Dutch form asked people to check a box if they would like to opt in to the organ donation program. The

Belgian form, by contrast, asked them to check a box if they would like to opt out. It turned out that the decision to check the box on either form was not made because people gave much thought to the organ donation question. They usually just left the box unchecked on both forms. Humans have an unconscious bias toward sticking with the status quo. When we are tasked with taking action to change the status quo vs. maintaining course, we will go with the path of least resistance. In this case, people just didn't want to go through the trouble of checking a box. When countries change their license forms to the "check this box to opt out" version of the question, organ donation consent skyrockets. It is the environment — the form, in this case — that is steering people to make an unconscious decision using a hidden heuristic.

Importantly, when you ask people why they made the decision to opt in (or not) to an organ donation program, they are wholly unaware of the unconscious thoughts that nudged them into action. "What happens is that people tell stories about why they made those decisions," Ariely told NPR's Guy Raz. "They portray them as — as if they spent the whole week on that decision. People who were in the opt-in form say things like, you know, I'm really worried about the medical system and whether some physicians will pull the plug a little too early if I do this. And people in the opt-out form say, you know, my parents raised me to be a caring, wonderful human being."[15]

These people are not lying. Their conscious minds are just searching for a *post hoc* explanation as to why they did what they did. But this is a delusion. "We usually think of ourselves as sitting in the driver's seat, with ultimate control over the decisions we make and the direction our life takes," Ariely writes in *Predictably Irrational*. "But, alas, this perception has more to do with our desires — with how we want to view ourselves — than with reality."

This organ donor story is particularly relevant to the problem of prognostic myopia. The question of what should happen to your liver or heart after you die requires you to engage in exceedingly complex thinking. You obviously have full-blown death wisdom. You are also being asked to predict not just how *you* would feel about donating your organs years or decades into the future (i.e., an ability to model future mental states), but also how *other* people will feel about this decision (e.g., the recipients of your organs) via theory of mind. The organ donation question requires the most complex matrix of human cognition and decision-making thrust onto that stage of consciousness we discussed in Chapter 5 that other animals lack.

And yet, our decision to donate our livers ultimately comes down to a single, unassuming too-lazy-to-tick -a-box heuristic that has little to do with all this complex cognition, and that never makes its way into conscious awareness. We are pushed into this decision by unseen forces in our minds. There are so many examples of research that reveal the hidden forces that control our decisions that it makes you wonder if humans have any free will at all. Here are three of my favorites:

Women will be more attracted to men who are not their sexual partner just after their ovaries release an egg, and before their period starts.[16] They will be even more attracted to these men if their current sexual partner has an asymmetrical face. So if you are a straight or bi lady who suddenly finds yourself attracted to your local Starbucks barista, it's not just because he's a fun conversationalist with a cute smile. It's because your current partner has a crooked nose and your body is trying to mate with someone more symmetrical.

If you are a white guy living in, say, New York City, and I ask you to look at a video screen and then record the speed at which you are able to recognize the image of a gun that is slowly coming into focus, you will do it faster if I first flash an image of a Black guy's face on-screen.[17] Even if the flash happens so fast that you are not consciously aware of it. Why? Because white guys who grow up in North America develop an unconscious bias that associates Black men with crime. This will be true even for white guys who swear that they don't have a racist bone in their body.

You are more likely to buy jam if you are looking at six varieties of jam stacked on a shelf than twenty-four varieties.[18] Why? Because human minds experience *choice overload* when there are too many options to consider. The more jams to choose from, the more likely we are to buy nothing. Our jam-buying decisions are often based on the configuration of the jam jars on the shelves, not the contents of the jam jars themselves.

I could go on citing these cognitive biases and acquired heuristics until the cows come home. But the take-home message is this: Even when we think our conscious decisions are arrived at via slow, deliberative, rational thinking, they are often the product of — or at least influenced by — a whole lot of unconscious processes bubbling away outside our awareness.

The fact that so much of human thinking and everyday decision-making is influenced by unconscious forces is important for understanding prognostic myopia. It drives home the point that our decisions are often the product of unseen emotions and heuristics in our minds, even if we are still consciously pondering a problem. And because these emotions and heuristics are designed exclusively for solving immediate — and not long-term future — problems, there is space for prognostic myopia to take root.

When we are faced with a decision involving the non-immediate future — whether it's an hour, tomorrow, or one year from now — our capacity for episodic foresight and temporal self-awareness allows us to project ourselves into that future. We can then imagine how we might feel based on the different choices we could make. But these far-future imagined scenarios, born of our uniquely human brand of cognition, do not carry the same emotional weight as those scenarios occurring in the immediate future. Being consciously aware of our hunger *right now* is what recruits that army of unconscious capacities that trigger our biases and heuristics to help us decide what to do in the present. Even though we can imagine being hungry five months from now, that army of unconscious capabilities is not exerting as much influence on our decision-making as it would if we were hungry *now*. These unconscious processes are not designed to understand the future. That's the paradox of prognostic myopia: We can imagine how we might feel in the future, but those feelings are not as meaningful to us as our current feelings. When episodic foresight steps onto that improv stage of subjective experience and gets broadcast to the subconscious parts of the mind, some of those parts simply don't understand what they are looking at. They are ancient processes evolved over the course of hundreds of millions of years to deal with the present. The distant future means nothing to them. So our capacity to understand the future and even envision ourselves in it is competing with decision-making systems whose component parts do not truly understand what they are being asked to do.

Now that we understand a bit more about how decision-making works for our species, and how prognostic myopia gets involved, it's time to see what happens when future-focused decision-making goes wrong.

The day-to-day problem of prognostic myopia

Prognostic myopia makes it difficult for us to make good decisions about our future because we're heavily influenced by our problems in the here and now. To see how this difficulty affects us on a day-to-day basis, I will provide examples from my life. I will compare the decisions I have made over the past forty-eight hours to the recommendations of a decision-making robot who always knows the optimal solution to all my problems. I am calling this robot Prognostitron. Let's say that Prognostitron's goal is to maximize my health and happiness, as well as the health and happiness of my future offspring. You'd think I would have that same goal, but as you will see from my actual decisions, that's clearly not the case.

Example number one: Justin wants to sing a song.

For a few years now, I have been getting together on a weekly basis with a few friends to play music. We are all middle-aged dads who were in rock bands in high school. It's the most cliché of all possible midlife crisis scenarios. At one of our recent practices we were really feeling the groove when ten-thirty p.m. rolled around. It was a school night for our kids, so none of us should really have been out past eleven, but we were having a blast. As we eyed our instrument cases and started to make a move to pack up, one of the lads asked: "Do we have time for one more song?"

Decision time. Now, Prognostitron would say that the only reasonable course of action would be to say no — to pack up my gear and be home in bed by eleven. My health and happiness levels will be maximized if I were to get a minimum of seven hours of sleep. That is an undeniable fact. So what did I do?

"Let's do one more song," I said.

In that moment, I was consciously aware of the right thing to do. But my mind was flooded with a ton of competing information — some of it unconscious — pushing me to stay. I was obviously enjoying myself, so my brain was keen to continue the endorphin hit that comes with singing nineties grunge music at the top of my lungs. But maybe I was also worried about disappointing the other guys if I were to leave early. My group in particular isn't prone to toxic peer pressure, but there's no escaping the deep-seated social concern that is fundamental to the human condition. My unconscious desire to maintain social bonds with my peers nudged me to stay. And then, of course, I had the ability to envision (via episodic foresight) what I would be like the next day if I decided to stay up past my bedtime: a grumpy, groggy mess. We all know this feeling — how many of us have stayed up to binge watch a show despite knowing we have to be up early the next morning? Despite my capacity for episodic foresight and the ability to understand — intellectually — that I would be tired, the fun I was having in that moment made it impossible for me to choose the best option.

And so, we played a couple more songs and I didn't get home until midnight. And I was a total wreck the next day. This is prognostic myopia in action: I was able to know exactly what staying up late would do to my future affective and physiological states on an intellectual level, but my mind justified doing the wrong thing because I couldn't feel the consequences of my actions in a way that was meaningful to my decision-making process. I knew intellectually that I would be tired. And when I woke up the next day, I was exactly that: tired. But, until that moment occurred, the full consequences of my decisions hadn't hit me.

Example number two: Justin wants to watch a Hallmark movie.

As a freelancer, I work from my home office most of the time. I do not have a boss looking over my shoulder making sure that I stay on task. I only have my own to-do lists and deadlines and a vague sense of "you should be doing something." In other words, self-discipline determines my productivity. Yesterday, however, I wasn't really feeling it. My procrastination levels were at an all-time high. To help me out of my funk, my wife asked if I might want to watch a Hallmark Christmas movie with her after lunch. Our relationship involves a lot of shared film-watching where we laugh ourselves silly at cinematic train wrecks. It's a surefire way to elevate my spirits, and she was right to suggest it.

I now had a decision to make: spend the afternoon

watching Netflix, or go back to work. Prognostitron would suggest the obvious answer: Go sit behind your computer and get some work done. The consequences of not doing so are potentially dire. Missing a deadline or disappointing a client who had hired me for a job could cause me to lose out on future gigs, which would cause serious emotional distress, not to mention financial hardship. It's a no-brainer: Skip the Hallmark movie and just go work.

So what did I choose to do? Obviously, I watched *A Christmas Prince*. Which, by the way, isn't a train wreck at all. Rose McIver is a delight, I tell you.

But how did I justify this? I knew just as well as Prognostitron what was at stake, and what the right thing to do was. But I also wanted to do something to remove the negative thoughts running through my head in that moment. And the easiest way to do that was to distract myself. And of course, watching a movie would mean spending quality time with my life partner, which is inherently rewarding. My mind was having a hard time balancing the need for immediate gratification with the long-term negative consequences of my decision. I was strangely indifferent to my future suffering, thanks to prognostic myopia.

Edward Wasserman and Thomas Zentall, two psychologists famous for their work with animal cognition, penned an essay in 2020 for NBC News trying to explain why humans like me are so bad at caring about the long-term consequences of our decisions:

Urgent survival needs (believed to be mediated by older brain systems that we share with many other animals) mean that we still engage in impulsive behaviors. And those behaviors, which once promoted our survival and reproductive success, are now suboptimal because we live in an environment in which long-term contingencies play an increasingly important part in our lives.[19]

This encapsulates why my daily life is so filled with prognostic myopia. But it also explains one of its far more sinister consequences. Because humans live in a world loaded with long-term contingencies, our poor decisions are not just affecting our daily lives. Humans alive today are making decisions whose negative consequences won't be felt by other humans until many years from now. Often, many *generations* into the future. Yet, we simply don't have minds designed to feel these consequences. In fact, in terms of decision-making, the further into the future we go, the less we care. To imagine a world three hundred years from now in which you are already dead removes even more of the emotional import that might be present in episodic foresight. We are no longer putting our temporal selves at the center of these time-traveling projections, but instead are trying to envision our hypothetical progeny walking through a nigh unimaginable hypothetical landscape. It simply becomes an intellectual exercise so far removed from the kinds of decisions our minds evolved to make. And this is how prognostic myopia might kill us.

The catastrophic future of prognostic myopia

The Global Challenges Foundation released a report in 2016 calculating that there is a "9.5% chance of human extinction within the next hundred years."[20] The three most likely ways were identified as: 1) nuclear holocaust, 2) climate change, and 3) ecological collapse.[21] Each of these is a result of human cognition bringing technologies into the world (e.g., nuclear weapons, combustion engines) that will damage the Earth in such a horrendous way that it can no longer sustain human life. It's not that we simply didn't understand the potential negative consequences of some of these technologies when they first arose. The quest to split the atom, for example, was undertaken specifically because we desired the negative consequence (i.e., wanted to invent bombs capable of killing millions of people in one go). Those responsible for creating nuclear weapons openly blamed (or maybe praised?) prognostic myopia for allowing them to do it. Robert Christy, one of the scientists with the Manhattan Project, once said: "I'd seen pictures of Hiroshima, of people who suffered very severe burns with flesh hanging in shreds from their arms. You don't think about those things when you're working on it. You think about solving the immediate problems."[22]

It's easy for us to shove those future-predicting cognitive skills off the stage of consciousness and instead direct our minds to dealing with problems in the now.

This capacity is closely related to the kind of denial that Ajit Varki suspects is vital to the human ability to compartmentalize thoughts of our own (and others') death. Denial helps us thrust these thoughts into the darkness of our unconscious and get on with the business of building a bomb.

Which brings us to the best example of the existential threat of prognostic myopia. It's a story of decision-making and denial that covers both the number two and number three most likely means of human extinction as pinpointed by the Global Challenges Foundation. And it involves a decision to bring something into the world with full knowledge of the destruction it would cause. I am talking, of course, about fossil fuels.

Let's start with this caveat. There was no single moment in recent history in which we switched from knowing that carbon emissions from the burning of fossil fuels *might* be causing climate change to being *sure* that they do. It took time for consensus to build. That being said, this is what we know about the oil industry's own understanding of its role in causing severe, extinction-level damage to the global environment. In 1968, Elmer Robinson and R. C. Robbins, two researchers from the Stanford Research Institute, presented a report to the American Petroleum Institute on atmospheric pollutants.[23] They took pains to include information about the dangers of carbon dioxide being released by the burning of fossil fuels. They warned that "CO_2 plays a significant role in establishing the thermal

214

balance of the earth" and that too much carbon dioxide in the atmosphere would result in a "green-house effect," which would result in "the melting of the Antarctic ice cap, a rise in sea levels, warming of the oceans and an increase in photosynthesis." They conclude that "man is now engaged in a vast geophysical experiment with his environment, the earth. Significant temperature changes are almost certain to occur by the year 2000 and these could bring about climatic changes," and that "there seems to be no doubt that the potential damage to our environment could be severe." In other words, Robinson and Robbins explained to the oil industry what the prevailing science at the time had concluded. None of this should come as any surprise — more than fifty years on, these findings are very much in the mainstream.

The oil industry, however, responded by not slowing the extraction of fossil fuels.

Ten years later, in 1978, the director of NASA's Institute for Space Studies, Dr. James Hansen, was called before the United States Senate Committee on Energy and Natural Resources. In his testimony, he confirmed to the US government — and the world — that what Robinson and Robbins had warned about was in fact an undeniable reality. He stated that "global warming has reached a level such that we can ascribe with a high degree of confidence a cause-and-effect relationship between the greenhouse effect and observed warming... In my opinion, the greenhouse effect has been detected, and it is changing our climate now." The cause, as

Hansen explained to the Senate, was carbon dioxide being released from burning fossil fuels.

The oil industry, however, responded once again by not slowing the extraction of fossil fuels.

In 2014, ExxonMobil released a report in which it stated that "ExxonMobil takes the risk of climate change seriously, and continues to take meaningful steps to help address the risk and to ensure our facilities, operations and investments are managed with this risk in mind."[24] It was widely reported as the first time that ExxonMobil acknowledged that climate change was "real," and that the fossil fuel industry had a part to play in setting things right.

The oil industry, however, responded — can you guess? — by not slowing the extraction of fossil fuels.

Why did the scientific evidence not sway people in the fossil fuel industry? Why has there been an overall annual increase in fossil fuel extraction since Robinson and Robbins's first report in 1968 that continues to this day?[25] If the stakes are so high — and we've known about them for so long — why didn't the industry act sooner? The answer is that at no time did the decision-makers in the fossil fuel industry feel a sense of urgency at each stage in which the problem was put before them. The problem they were being asked to consider involved the far future. One hundred years down the road. A time when they would be long dead. Besides, in terms of their immediate interests, how much wealth has been generated from the fossil fuel industry? How many millionaires or billionaires has it made? How many jobs has it created? Our present and immediate future prosperity is predicated on the proliferation of cars, trains, and airplanes, all of which run on what the oil industry makes. This is prognostic myopia in action. They could just ignore the evidence, however damning, because they were focused on the immediate problem (and immediate benefits). Just like Robert Christy did when tinkering away on the A-bomb. Of course, sometimes they did more than just ignore; sometimes they actively obfuscated the truth. The (now former) Senior Director of Federal Relations at Exxon Mobil Corporation Keith McCoy was caught on tape in July 2021 admitting that the company had done just that. "Did we fight aggressively against some of the science? Yes. Did we join some of these shadow groups to work against some of the early efforts? Yes, that's true. But there's nothing illegal about that. You know, we were looking out for our investments, we were looking out for our shareholders."

However, I don't see Keith McCoy as a mustache-twirling villain as much as I see him as a victim of prognostic myopia. Like most humans, he's not equipped to truly feel what it will be like to experience the future consequences of his current actions. None of us are. And consequently, our social, financial, and political systems reflect this fact. "Our political-legal system was developed to address structured, short-term, direct cause and effect issues (the exact opposite of the climate issue)," suggested the 2020 Global Catastrophic Risks report.[26]

Which explains why both governments and businesses are so slow to act when looking at reports forecasting our impending extinction. We've built our societies on the scaffolding of prognostic myopia.

But there are the occasional people who do seem to fully feel the distant future, and who are trying their darndest to nudge the political-legal systems into action. Greta Thunberg, for example. In her speech to the World Economic Forum's Annual Meeting in Davos in January 2020, as part of her *skolstrejk för klimatet* campaign, she spoke like someone whose brain is overcome with a sense of fear in the here and now when envisioning future scenarios:

> We all have a choice. We can create transformational action that will safeguard the living conditions for future generations. Or we can continue with our business as usual and fail. We must change almost everything in our current societies. I want you to panic. I want you to feel the fear I feel every day. And then I want you to act. I want you to act as you would in a crisis. I want you to act as if our house is on fire. Because it is.[27]

Clearly, our species is not acting as if our house is on fire. Despite the widespread awareness of climate change as a real problem caused by human carbon emissions, and despite the fact that nations and world leaders have

promised to curb emissions and done things like sign
the Paris Agreement (which aims to reduce global greenhouse gas emissions), the reality is that we, all over the
planet, are only increasing the amount of carbon we're
releasing. Greenhouse gas emissions are on track to rise
by 16 percent by 2030.[28] This will cause global atmospheric temperature to increase by 2.7 degrees Celsius
by the end of the century. An increase of this magnitude
will result in severe floods, crop failures, heavy rainfall,
heat waves, and wildfires that will render most of the
planet uninhabitable.[29] The increase has already begun
to hurt the world's most vulnerable populations. Which
is exactly why there is that 9.5 percent chance of human
extinction within a hundred years. However dire,
thanks to prognostic myopia, it doesn't look like there's
enough political will to stop it from happening. Which
is why Greta called out world leaders again at the Youth-
4Climate summit in Milan, Italy, in September 2021:

> Build back better. Blah, blah, blah. Green economy.
> Blah blah blah. Net zero by 2050. Blah, blah, blah.
> This is all we hear from our so-called leaders. Words
> that sound great but so far have not led to action.
> Our hopes and ambitions drown in their empty
> promises. They've now had 30 years of blah, blah,
> blah and where has that led us? We can still turn this
> around — it is entirely possible. It will take immedi-
> ate, drastic annual emission reductions. But not if

things go on like today. Our leaders' intentional lack of action is a betrayal toward all present and future generations.[30]

Prognostic myopia clearly affects our world leaders as well as all of us. Nobody is immune to the cognitive dissonance it generates. Even when the stakes are as high as global extinction. Consider that a child born today is five times more likely to die in a global extinction event than in a car crash. Think about that for a second. Think about how often people drive, and then read that sentence again. Yet, if I am being honest, I cannot personally *feel* that danger at all.

If you told me that if I continued to drive my daughter to school every day, there was a 9.5 percent chance that she would die in a car crash, I would almost certainly find alternate means as quickly as I could. I can feel that danger deep in my bones. But if you told me that if I continued to drive my daughter to school, there was a 9.5 percent chance that my great-great-granddaughter would die from ecological collapse, would I stop driving? No. Even though that's what awaits my family in the future, here I am, driving my Subaru around like everything is fine.

Humans simply do not have the ability to evaluate the consequences of our actions in the long term using the same criteria we use for short-term decisions. What about Greta? Why is she unique, or seemingly unique, compared to so many of us? Greta has credited her autism with giving her an ability to stay focused on future problems and not be distracted by the pull of prognostic myopia.[31] "I have Aspergers and that means I'm sometimes a bit different from the norm," she tweeted. "And — given the right circumstances — being different is a superpower."[32] Other than a handful of prescient exceptions, we, as a species, are not designed to feel that way about our decisions. Many of us do not have super-powers like Greta; we are, simply, crippled with prog-nostic myopia.

I would like to take a moment to directly address those of you who might be reading these words at the turn of the millennium, including my own great-great-grandchildren. On behalf of my generation, I apologize. I was born in the 1970s and came of age during the industrial and capitalist boom that gripped North America in the '80s and '90s. There was almost no discussion about how our behavior might affect the health of the Earth. Although plenty of scientists talked about things like "recycling" or "acid rain" or "global warming" at the time, everyday folks didn't really get into the whole climate change thing until it became clear — at the turn of the current millennium — that we were headed down a dark path. I also want to personally say sorry: I keep driving around in my Subaru despite knowing exactly what this means to you.

As humans, we are victims of our own success. There

has never been a species on this planet capable of fundamentally transforming the Earth's environment like we have. Now, then, comes the time for putting everything into perspective. With the specter of prognostic myopia looming darkly over us, it is time to determine the value of human intelligence.

Chapter 7

Human Exceptionalism

Are we winning?

The sciences must now pave the way for the future
task of the philosopher; this task being understood
to mean that the philosopher must solve the problem of value; that he has to determine the hierarchy
of values.

— Nietzsche[1]

Eric Barcia had carefully calculated the height of the
railroad trestle at Lake Accotink Park in Springfield,
Virginia. It was seventy feet from the trestle's edge to
the concrete spillway below. An amateur bungee enthu-
siast who had been described by his grandmother as
"very smart in school,"[2] Barcia taped together a bunch
of bungee cords until he had created a single cord that
was about 70 feet long. In the early morning of July 12,

1997, Barcia fastened the makeshift cord to his ankles, tied the other end to the trestle, and leapt off the bridge.

His body was found by a jogger soon after. Since bungee cords stretch when pulled (a fact that Barcia had overlooked), he had overestimated the length of cord by some sixty feet.

The temptation here is to snicker at Barcia's stupidity. But this is not a story of stupidity. Barcia's cord-length miscalculation was but a sad footnote to a much larger tale of human cognitive prowess. To stand on the edge of that trellis and devise such an elaborate plan is a testament to everything amazing about the human mind. His death was the result of a simple mathematical error. Even hyper-intelligent rocket scientists make similar mistakes. Remember when the $125 million Mars Climate Orbiter burned up in the atmosphere of the red planet back in 1999? The engineers at NASA's Jet Propulsion Laboratory used the metric system to calculate the orbiter's trajectory, but the engineers at Lockheed Martin Astronautics (who built the orbiter's software) used inches, feet, and pounds. The result? As it entered orbit, the space probe was 170 kilometers too low. Like Barcia, it plunged unceremoniously to its death, a tragic end to an otherwise remarkable tale of human ingenuity.

The goal of this book has been to determine what stories like Barcia's tell us about the value of human intelligence. Since the first chapter, I've been cataloging the cognitive skills that fall under the umbrella of intelligence to determine if the human mind is exceptional and/or a good thing. Alternatively, would we be better off (both as individuals and as a species) with the mind of some other animal?

Let's take a closer look at our amateur bungee jumper. What exactly was happening in his mind that ultimately led to his death? Barcia had clearly been planning his jump for days — maybe even weeks — in advance. Which means that he, unlike most other animal species, was able to envision a version of himself in a future scenario wherein he would experience a positive feeling (e.g., joy, fear, excitement) as a result of jumping off the bridge. In other words, exactly what you would expect from an adrenaline junkie. The plan itself involved an intimate knowledge of cause and effect — a form of causal inference that is the hallmark of our species. Most animals understand that things fall down, but Barcia had a deeper knowledge of tension loads, trajectories, classical mechanics, and so forth. He knew, for example, that tying a cord around his ankles would prevent him from crashing into the ground. And, of course, Barcia was perfectly aware that jumping off a 70-foot-tall bridge — under any circumstances — is inherently dangerous and thus scary. But, as any thrill-seeker will tell you, overriding this fear is part of the fun. After all, he was bungee jumping, not trying to kill himself. Everything we've discussed throughout this book about the human mind's uniqueness is apparent here.

Now imagine that Santino — the rock-throwing chimpanzee we met in Chapter 3 — was standing next to

Barcia on the trestle's edge. What is the difference between Santino's and Barcia's thought processes in that moment? Since chimpanzees are our closest evolutionary relative, comparing how Santino and Barcia would approach this scenario will give us important clues about human exceptionalism and our minds compared to other animals. Santino, for the record, would never tie a rope around his ankles and fling himself off a railroad trestle in pursuit of an endorphin rush.

Let's begin with the basics: Do nonhuman animals even engage in thrill-seeking behavior? Many species of animals engage in novelty-seeking behavior — a close cousin of thrill-seeking. Consider cats. YouTube is filled with examples of cats getting themselves into dangerous spots because of their love of exploring potentially dangerous scenarios (e.g., tall trees, tight spaces). But the clearest example of not just novelty-seeking but full on thrill-seeking in animals is found in the wild macaques of India seen in the 2017 BBC production *Spy in the Wild*.[3] These monkeys climb a fifteen-foot pillar perched above an outdoor fountain, flinging themselves into the narrow pool where even a slight miscalculation could cause them serious injury or death if they fail to hit the water. Although far less dangerous than jumping off a seventy-foot bridge above a concrete road, there is no denying that these monkeys are engaging in a dangerous activity from which they derive pleasure despite (or because of) the risks involved.

So, what's stopping Santino from bungee jumping?

It's possible — if not likely — that a chimpanzee would want to engage in dangerous thrill-seeking behavior similar to the pool-diving macaques. But bungee jumping and pool diving are not identical when it comes to the cognitive skills needed to experience the thrill. Santino would need to come up with a plan involving the assembly of materials to create a bungee cord that would take days to execute — involving mental time travel skills that he does not likely possess. He would also need a sophisticated grasp of cause and effect — an understanding of what happens to a falling object that is secured to another object via an elastic material. He would then need to assemble this sophisticated kind of tool and find a way to secure it to himself and the bridge; skills that are seemingly well above his pay grade. This is a kind of why specialism that chimpanzees lack. Even if Santino had bungee-jumping aspirations, he is just not intelligent enough to bungee jump.

But that's a good thing. Barcia's bungee plan was a case of complex human cognition gone wrong. His intelligence, not his stupidity, was directly responsible for his death. Santino, the less intelligent of the two on paper, behaved more intelligently *precisely because* he was less intelligent. In other words, intelligence sometimes results in very stupid behavior.

Consider this example of a human versus animal battle of the wits that highlights the pitfalls — or perhaps impotence — of human intelligence. There are three species of bedbugs that feed on humans when we are sleeping (i.e., *Cimex lectularius, Cimex hemipterus,* and *Leptocimex boueti*).[4] Bedbugs are attracted to our body heat, our body odor, and the carbon dioxide we exhale when we breathe.[5] They're weirdly flat insects, which helps them hide in places we'd never think to look. They can slide in between cracks as small as the thickness of a sheet of paper. And because they feed exclusively on our blood, they find hiding places near where we sleep. They like us best when we are motionless in bed — an easier target. Their entire biology is centered around reading human behavior to try to figure out when we're at our most vulnerable. "They won't come out to feed until you let your guard down," explained Dr. Jody Green to me over Zoom. Jody is the urban entomologist extension educator with the University of Nebraska-Lincoln, and an expert in the behavior of the insects that drive us crazy: bedbugs, head lice, termites, fleas, etc. "They learn your schedule. If you work nights and only sleep during the day, they adapt — they get on your sleep schedule. If you go on vacation, they can wait for you to get back."

Bedbugs' hiding strategies can get quite elaborate. As they age, bedbugs shed their exoskeletons, which they leave behind as a ghostly shell. When you spray your house with pesticides, young bedbugs will sometimes sprint toward the nearest exoskeleton left behind by a larger adult and hide inside as the pesticides pass over them. "For extra protection," explained Jody.

But bedbugs' main strategy is to hide in the places

that nobody looks or thinks to spray with poison. Think about a hotel room for a moment. It gets a thorough scrubbing every day, including changing the bedding. And yet, hotel rooms are notorious hot spots for bedbugs. That's because hotel rooms, just like our homes, have plenty of locations that are overlooked when it comes to regular cleaning. Some items rarely get washed. Things like the curtains. Or bed skirts. Which are often riddled with bedbugs.

Maybe the craftiest hiding spot in a hotel is the one that you are the least likely to disturb: the Bible in the nightstand. Nearly every hotel room in North America has one thanks to a campaign by the Gideons International: a Christian evangelical group that has been distributing free Bibles for more than a century. The Bible has hundreds of pages between which a flat bedbug can slip. It's the perfect hideout for an entire civilization of bedbugs. If you're doing a sweep of your hotel room to check for bedbugs, this is the first place you should look, suggests Jody. "I know it's probably not good to go flipping through the Bible looking for bedbugs, but..."

Bedbugs can generate these elaborate hiding strategies using, as we have seen in previous chapters, relatively simple decision-making skills that do not avail of things like episodic foresight or causal inference. And yet, these simple minds regularly outwit our complex human minds in a hide-and-seek battle. But this is not the most important lesson from this story. Because bedbugs are so difficult to find and squish, humans have been forced to unleash our most sophisticated why specialist abilities to come up with solutions for killing them.[6] The chemical dichlorodiphenyltrichloroethane — more commonly known as DDT — is a potent insecticide, originally used to kill mosquitoes, and deployed widely during the Second World War to stop the spread of mosquito-borne diseases like malaria and typhoid. But it's equally as effective at killing bedbugs. After the war ended, DDT became commercially available in North America, and average citizens started spraying it around their homes with wild abandon. With good reason. In the early 1900s, every single home in the United States had experienced a bedbug infestation. Within a decade, though, and before we learned how bad it was for human health,[7] the mass spraying of DDT in North America almost led to the eradication of the bedbug on the continent. Almost.

The bedbugs that survived this purge were the ones that had developed a resistance to DDT. While the humans were taking their victory lap, these resistant bedbugs began to multiply — slowly at first. But then by the 1990s, the bedbug population exploded. By the mid-2000s, every state in the US was infested. A 2018 report found that 97 percent of pest control companies in the US treated for bedbugs within the previous year.[8] In other words, DDT-resistant bedbugs are everywhere these days. In fact, modern bedbugs are resistant to almost every pesticide out there. So in the end, our smartest solutions were still no match for the simple minds of bedbugs. But there's even more to this story, which highlights the grand downfall of the human mind thanks to prognostic myopia.

It turns out that releasing huge amounts of DDT into the environment in our fight against bedbugs was a rather boneheaded solution. It has made its way into the very fabric of our lives in ways we are only just now starting to appreciate. Even though the United States banned the use of DDT in 1972, every single person living in the US right now (including children born after the ban) has trace amounts of DDT in their bodies.[9] DDT has a half-life in water of 150 years,[10] which means that the DDT coating the floors and walls of the homes we sprayed for bedbugs in the 1940s would have ended up in perfectly stable condition in our mop-bucket water. When those buckets were emptied, the DDT hitched a ride with the wastewater into sewage treatment plants, or straight into our rivers and oceans, where it began building up inside the bodies of fish and other aquatic animals. Some of those DDT-soaked fish ended up on our dinner plates, causing the chemical to build up in our own tissues, where it stays until we die. Mothers can pass traces of DDT on to their children through breastmilk, making it all but impossible to avoid ingesting DDT even today. What's worse, DDT has induced epigenetic changes in women exposed to the chemical that are being passed down to their children and grandchildren. And these changes are directly linked to an increase in obesity, which is correlated with an increase in breast cancer in women whose ancestral line was exposed to DDT.[11] "What your great-grandmother was exposed to during pregnancy, like DDT, may promote a dramatic increase in your susceptibility to obesity, and you will pass this on to your grandchildren in the absence of any continued exposures," said Michael Skinner, an epigenetics expert from Washington State University.[12] Not only are humans losing the bedbug war, but our hyper-intelligent technological solutions for fighting them has resulted in us poisoning ourselves and our grandchildren.

This is the problem with thinking of human intelligence as something special, and assuming that specialness is a good thing. Human cognition and animal cognition are not all that different, but where human cognition is more complex, it does not always produce a better outcome. In both the Barcia versus Santino and the bedbugs versus DDT battles, complex, human-style thinking was the loser. This is what I call the *Exceptionalism Paradox*. It's the idea that even though humans are indeed exceptional when it comes to our cognition, it does not mean we are better at the game of life than other animals. In fact, because of this paradox, humans might be a less successful species precisely because of our amazing, complex intelligence.

F*ck complexity

What exactly is "success" when we're talking about evolution? Evolutionary success could mean that a species has remained relatively the same for a long period of time due to its effective biological design. Or it could mean that it has spread out across the globe in huge numbers. By either definition, if you want to look at examples of "evolutionary success" in the animal kingdom, it's simple cognition — not complex, humanlike cognition — that wins every time. Let's talk about your colon for a second. You might already be aware that the human body is stuffed with (and covered in) bacteria. In fact, your body is home to equal parts bacteria and human cells; you have about 38 trillion of each.[13] Bacteria cells are an order of magnitude smaller than human cells, which is why it looks and feels as if you are mostly human. But you're not. You're half-human at best. Most of these bacteria live in your colon. Every time you poop, you discharge billions of bacteria; half of your poo is comprised of bacterial cells.[14] In fact, there are more bacteria in your morning poop than there are humans alive on this planet. There are five million trillion trillion bacteria cells alive on Earth right now — that's more bacteria than stars in the universe.[15] Just based on numbers, it's clear that bacteria are the most successful life-form that has ever lived. And they are, by any stretch of the imagination, a life-form devoid of anything in the way of complex cognition.

But even if we put aside the obvious champions of evolution (e.g., prokaryotes like bacteria) in terms of numbers, and look instead at which species have been around the longest in their current form, we find again that simple thinking outperforms complex cognition, even when it comes to larger, brainier, vertebrate species. Consider crocodilians. The ancestors to crocodiles, alligators, caimans, and so forth, first appeared about ninety-five million years ago — in the middle of the Cretaceous period.[16] That means that crocodiles were sunning themselves along riverbanks as T. rex, velociraptors, triceratops, and all the other species from *Jurassic Park* sauntered by. The crocodilians handily survived the global mass extinction event that killed off three-quarters of all species on Earth, including the dinosaurs.

Crocodilians are perhaps the most successful large vertebrate species that has ever lived. And yet, crocodilians, like most reptiles, don't have much of a reputation for complex cognition. Although they exhibit play behavior[17] and even use tools,[18] they are not prodigal problem solvers. They don't exhibit anything in the way of episodic foresight, causal inference, theory of mind, or any of those hard-hitting skills we find in humans. This might be due to a sampling bias; there are no crocodile cognition labs that I know of. I can't imagine too many university research labs willing to let a bunch of psychology undergrads stuff a crocodile into an fMRI machine. But it wouldn't matter. Crocodiles are getting by just fine without any of these cognitive skills. Because sometimes less is more, cognitively speaking.

To understand evolution's indifference to complexity, consider the plight of the sea squirt. Sea squirts are a marine animal from the subphylum Tunicata. There are around 2,150 different species. In their larval stage, they look a lot like a tadpole. They have a head and a tail, and a spinal cord with a little miniature brain that helps them swim around. Once they reach maturity, they cement themselves onto a piece of rock. They then digest their brain and spinal cord and spend the rest of their life on that rock, filter feeding. This is natural selection concluding that the best path to success for a sea squirt is to actively remove any chance of *thinking at all*. Because, as I've argued for humans, complex cognition can be an existential liability.

The simple organisms (from bacteria to sea squirts to crocodiles) have been winning the natural selection game for millions of years without any need for complex cognition. Which goes to show that simple cognitive traits — like the boring old associative learning we find in bedbugs — have an unbeatable track record when it comes to generating successful behavior. Lucy the dog from Chapter 1 used associative learning to understand that the shaking alder branches we saw during our walk in the woods could indicate danger. She and I both froze in place upon seeing those branches. My why specialist abilities might have given me a deeper understanding of the reason the branches moved, but the subsequent behavior Lucy and I displayed was identical. Natural selection doesn't care about the level of complexity that gave rise to our vigilance, only whether it is effective at keeping us alive.

Our human causal inferential abilities seem impressive, and being a why specialist has helped us achieve so much, but causal inference is the new kid on the block. It will need to stick around for a good billion years before we can consider it a robust cognitive solution that could rival associative learning. And since prognostic myopia has put our species in imminent risk of extinction (e.g., via climate change, nuclear war, or ecological collapse), it's exceedingly unlikely that our species is going to be around for another millennium, let alone another billion years. Those ancient cave paintings of therianthropes in Sulawesi have become a prophetic symbol of our own fate; they are evidence of our complex thinking about morality and the meaning of life. And yet, the paintings themselves are beginning to vanish. After surviving for forty thousand years, they are now being rapidly destroyed, flaking away due to droughts and high temperatures brought on by human-induced climate change.[19]

Barcia, then, is the ultimate symbol for our species as it relates to the Exceptionalism Paradox. It was his human brand of exceptional cognitive complexity that led to his removal from the gene pool. We are cursed by prognostic myopia and seemingly preoccupied with tying the bungee cord of self-extinction around our ankles. In the grand scheme of things, we are destined to vanish from the Earth long before either bacteria or crocodiles. It's a dark and cheerless way of looking at things. And maybe not the grand conclusion you were hoping for. Luckily, not everyone agrees with my bleak assessment of the value of human intelligence.

#winning

My friend Brendan is a journalist who is not shy when it comes to picking apart arguments or challenging ideas. We meet regularly at a diner for breakfast where we drink too much coffee and rant about our passions and problems. After a long discussion about why the Danish prime minister Birgitte Nyborg's husband was such an unsympathetic character in season 1 of *Borgen,* we wandered into the topic of human intelligence. I argued that *intelligence* is a value-laden term that we should eighty-six altogether, and instead simply catalog and describe individual cognitive skills without judgment. If we judge the value of cognition not by its complexity but by biological success, then humans are both too new on the scene to properly evaluate, and likely to run afoul of natural selection due to prognostic myopia. Crocodiles might be a better candidate for the moniker of *intelligent animal* if we're valuing cognition for its ability to generate evolutionarily advantageous behavior.

"In that sense, crocodiles are winning," I said.

"No. We won," argues Brendan. "No other animal has dominated as hard as we have."

"What do you mean by *dominated*?" I countered. "Because there are more bacteria living in your butt right now than there are humans living on Earth. If we're judging 'dominance' on sheer numbers, bacteria are winning."

"Bacteria might be plentiful," argued Brendan, "but

they can't have this conversation. We can reflect on our own lives and bacteria and crocodiles can't. We've gone above and beyond simply finding food and shelter. How are we not winning? I have always taken for granted that we're winning. Because look at what we're doing!"

Brendan then went on to cite example after example of our species' greatest achievements: space exploration, splitting the atom, vaccines, legal systems, mega-cities, industrialized food production, the internet, music, art, poetry, theater, literature, etc. This list of things that humans can create that other animals cannot is mind-blowingly long. All of it built on the back of our capacity for language, culture, science, math, and so forth. I argued that none of it really matters, that it's all just noise. In the billion-year history of animal cognition, these achievements are just flashes in the pan — bright, smoky footnotes to a much longer story about the dominance of simple minds.

"That's bullshit," Brendan said.

Am I seriously arguing that these kind of achievements — like walking on the moon — have no real value? If we don't attribute value to biological success in terms of either a numbers game (i.e., how many individuals of our species are alive right now), or a longevity game (i.e., how long our species has existed and is likely to continue existing), what other way do we have to judge the value of our cognition and the behavior it generates? Is our exceptional ability to understand and manipulate the physical properties of the universe something that is *inherently* good? That's what Brendan is suggesting. He is wrestling with a concept of value untethered to biology, where the pursuit of knowledge, truth, and beauty is a worthy goal on its own. I, on the other hand, am determining value from the standpoint of fitness. To me, Copernicus and Ada Lovelace are shining beacons of the awesomeness of human intellectual achievement, but don't account for much if our species goes extinct after just 300,000 years. For Brendan, living a billion years splashing about in the water like a crocodile is worthless if it's not going to result in a Copernicus or a Lovelace cropping up to help unravel the secrets of the universe.

I think there is middle ground here. I think there is a method for determining value that melds Brendan's philosophical bent with my coldhearted scientism. And, like everything in my life these days, it all comes back to my chickens.

What matters matters

What is the value of human intelligence? There are a few things that humans do that other species cannot, which is what generates that long list of human accomplishments that Brendan championed, and which are the result of our unique cognition. I've grappled with the problem of what *good* is supposed to mean in reference to those accomplishments, and concluded that cognitive things that are *good* are the ones that generate the largest amount of pleasure for both the individual animal, and the world at large, both now and in the foreseeable future. For me, this middle ground for determining what constitutes "success" makes the most sense. I don't think success should be grounded in either a numbers game (e.g., how many individual humans there are) or a longevity game (e.g., how long crocodilians have been around) for this reason: The Earth is going to get swallowed by the sun in a few billion years. That's a fact. Before that happens, there will be millions of new species formed from weirdo selection pressures that we can't conceive of. Maybe humans will go extinct and be replaced by a giant crow species with prehensile tails, full-blown theory of mind, and a ravenous desire for space exploration. Who knows? Does it matter? The sun will eventually destroy these new über-crows along with every living thing on the planet, so what does all this talk of population numbers or biological longevity really matter in the long term? The value of life then must be framed in the here and now. And what matters most to you, me, or any animal species alive at this very moment is pleasure.

Every living thing exists for a blink of life. And in that blink, if it's lucky enough to have a brain, it will float from day to day on a cushion of qualia. It is qualia that fuel life, and push animals to behave, think, and be. They matter to us, so they matter. We can rejigger the question of value away from notions of domination and have it apply to the one thing that seems universal: the pursuit of positive qualia. In other words, the pursuit of pleasure. I think both Brendan and I can agree that the one thing that all animals value is the maximization of pleasure and the minimization of misery.

From a biological perspective, this pleasure-maximization idea makes sense insofar as the job of brains is to produce behavior that will help an animal survive and reproduce. Therefore, a brain will create pleasure qualia to let the animal know that it's on the right track. The animal behavior researcher Jonathan Balcombe explores this idea in his book *Pleasurable Kingdom:*

> The animal world is teeming with an enormous variety of breathing, sensing, feeling creatures who are not merely alive, but living life. Each is trying to get along — to feed and shelter themselves, to reproduce, to seek what is good and avoid what is bad. There's a diversity of good things to be gotten: food, water, movement, rest, shelter sunshine, shade, discovery, anticipation, social interaction, play and sex. And because gaining these goods is adaptive, evolution has equipped animals with the capacity to experience their rewards. Like us, they are pleasure seekers.[20]

Pleasure qualia are the drivers of evolution. Pleasure is both intrinsically rewarding to the brain experiencing it, and biologically rewarding in that it inspires animals to pursue goals that increase their biological fitness. From an ethical perspective, you could argue that behaviors that produce the greatest pleasure in the world to the greatest number of conscious beings are the ones that carry the most value. The human achievements that Brendan listed (e.g., vaccines, farming) do exactly that, which is why Brendan considers them inherently valuable.

This pleasure-focused value is old-school ethics stuff. Pleasure is the beating heart of utilitarian philosophies first described by Jeremy Bentham and John Stuart Mill more than two centuries ago.[21] Bentham described his pleasure-based utilitarian moral philosophy as follows:

> Nature has placed mankind under the governance of two sovereign masters, pain and pleasure. It is for them alone to point out what we ought to do, as well as to determine what we shall do. On the one hand the standard of right and wrong, on the other the chain of causes and effects, are fastened to their throne. They govern us in all we do, in all we say, in all we think: every effort we can make to throw off our subjection, will serve but to demonstrate and confirm it.[22]

Slap together this utilitarianism with the biological value of qualia, and you have a system for judging which animals are, as Brendan says, #winning. The winning species are the ones that can live their lives having experienced the most amount of pleasure. Unfortunately, if we rebrand success as the ability to generate pleasure in the world, then humans still run afoul of the Exception-alism Paradox.

Consider language, one of the cognitive skills that Brendan singled out as part and parcel of what makes humans so special. Indeed, this is a behavior that knows no equal in nonhuman species. Like all cognitive skills, the building blocks of language can be found in the communication systems of many other species, from the referential calls of prairie dogs that can describe the size, color, and species of animal that they see,[23] to the complex structure of bird or whale song that we can sense is a rudimentary form of grammar.[24] But there is no species other than humans that has a generative grammar system capable of combining meaningful word elements into sentences that can represent any and every idea that pops into our heads.

The first question is, do we, as a species, experience more pleasure from our use of language than the non-linguistic animals with whom we share this planet? On one hand, language can be used to create songs, jokes, and stories that are, in my life, perhaps the single largest source of pleasure I experience on a regular basis. My chickens will never know this pleasure. But does that make them less happy? This is a tricky question. Chickens did not evolve to use language, in the same way that humans did not evolve to roost. Is my life impoverished because I don't sleep on a branch at night? Clearly not. My biology is not designed for roosting. It is, however, designed to learn and use language, and I would very likely lead a much sadder life had I grown up without any exposure to it. Chickens, then, do not know what they are missing because they are not designed to miss it. Their pleasure is drawn from scratching the ground and eating larvae. They would draw no similar pleasure from watching an episode of *Borgen*. Thus, there is no reason to assume a net loss in pleasure for our nonlinguistic animal brethren.

But there might be a net loss for humans precisely because of our language capacity. Chapter 2 explored the human capacity for deception, which accelerates with language. Our ability to lie and deceive, to convince and cajole, is partly responsible for all the evil in this world. Linguistic aptitude can be what gives tyrants and leaders their power; think of the influence Hitler's speeches (and Nietzsche's writings) had in driving the rise of Nazism in Germany. And even when leaders are not particularly eloquent, their words convey ideas that drive nations forward toward jingoistic and genocidal goals that result in the suffering and death of millions. As much as language is responsible for the glorious achievements of our species (e.g., culture, art, science), it is also to blame for its ability to spread misery and destruction. Without language and the underlying sociocognitive skills that make it possible, it is unlikely that my chickens will ever unite *en masse* to rain death down upon the world in pursuit of glory for the Great Chicken Nation.

Like most human cognitive achievements, language is a double-edged sword responsible for as much misery as pleasure. Would we, as a species, be happier without it? Quite possibly. Would the world have experienced as much death and misery had humans remained a nonlinguistic ape? Probably not. Language might generate more misery than pleasure for the animal kingdom as a whole. Language falls victim to the Exceptionalism Paradox: It is the ultimate symbol of the uniqueness of the human mind, and yet despite its wondrousness, it has helped generate more misery for the creatures on this planet (including ourselves) than pleasure.

What about our capacity for science and math? Like language, our mathematical competencies have roots that run deep in the minds of all animals. Spotted hyenas can count how many individuals there are in rival hyena groups, which helps them decide whether it's worth getting into a fight.[25] A newborn guppy is able to count to at least three, preferring to join a group of three fish over two, a handy skill when there is safety in numbers.[26] Honeybees can count the number of landmarks they fly over on their way from the hive to a food source, helping them find their way back to a yummy flower patch by, for example, tallying up the number of houses there are along the way.[27] But humans have taken these mathematical competencies to a new level. Einstein's field equation explaining how space-time is warped by gravity might have its roots in a numerical ability common to hyenas and honeybees, but that resemblance is about as strong as my cinnamon-scented candle's resemblance to the sun.

Science operates on a similarly sophisticated level. It's our why specialist capacity for causal inference on steroids. The scientific method gives us the tools to test hypotheses and uncover cause-and-effect relationships that have given us paradigm-altering ideas like germ theory or quantum mechanics. Our collective culture is built on the back of science and math, and the modern world exists because of these skills. And these skills simply do not exist in nonhuman animals in anything but the most basic form.

So does science and math generate an abnormal amount of pleasure for our species? Arguably, yes. While science and math have brought us death and destruction (e.g., atom bombs), it is also responsible for modern medicine and food production. So, on average, we have seen a spike in pleasure — as a species — because of it. And that spike might then mean that our daily lives are slightly less misery-filled than that of other species. They may spend more time struggling to find food and shelter and fight off disease than your average human.

But then again, science and math *did* bring us that atom bomb, and the mechanized farming practices that brought us a grocery store full of bananas, but also an atmosphere full of carbon. So it's not all good. Like language, it is a double-edged sword. The average human might be better off now than we were 100,000 years ago thanks to our technical and scientific discoveries, but the planet itself (and the creatures on it) is far worse off. There is far less pleasure for the million species currently threatened with extinction thanks mostly to human behavior.[28] And, if we wind up going extinct by the end of the century (for which there is that 9.5 percent chance of happening), then all that net gain in pleasure will have been for nothing. Our capacity for scientific thinking and mathematical competencies are another fantastic example of the Exceptionalism Paradox: awesome and awful in equal measure.

The final verdict

Are humans winning in the sense that we both produce and experience more pleasure — on average — than other species? Before I answer that, we need to have a frank discussion about this idea of "average." I am not an average human. As a middle-aged white male living in a country that ranks near the top of health, education, and standard of living indices, my lifestyle is privileged to an absurd degree. I can lounge around sipping my imported coffee, watching my hobby chickens roam my yard without any worry about where my next meal will come from. This is not normal. At the moment, one in four people living on this planet are experiencing moderate to severe food insecurity, meaning that they do not have the means to acquire enough food for a healthy diet, or have run out of food altogether.[29] Despite the falling rates of food insecurity since the start of the millennium, it is still quite normal for the average human to not have enough food to eat. In Canada, my life expectancy is 82.4 years, nearly a decade more than the average global life expectancy of 72.6. And almost thirty years more than the Central African Republic, which has the lowest life expectancy at just fifty-three years.[30] The average human living in the Central African Republic, which has been beset by a civil war since 2012 and where 2.5 million people out of a population of 4.6 million need humanitarian relief,[31] is leading a very different life from my own. I would wager that moments of pleasure and happiness are exceedingly rare for every one of the fourteen thousand child soldiers in the Central African Republic. The "average" human, then, is living a much more difficult and less pleasure-filled life than I am. Because of the paradox of human intelligence, we have created a world in which there are extremes in terms of pleasure maximalization (on my end) and pleasure deficit (as we see in the Central African Republic right now). One's own privilege must be considered when having breakfast conversations about the value of the human experience.

Here, then, is the final verdict. *Homo sapiens* are no more likely to experience pleasure — on average — than other species. Whatever gifts our capacity for language, math, science, etc. have given us, there is no evidence to suggest that my life — as privileged as it is — is filled with more pleasure than the lives of my chickens.

Not even the happiest of humans can necessarily out-happy my chickens. Consider the life of a Buddhist monk who spends their day in quiet contemplation, having mastered the ability to minimize the discomfort felt by negative thoughts or emotions. Matthieu Ricard, for example, is a Tibetan Buddhist monk considered to be the world's happiest person. On his best day, let's say that Ricard experiences only pleasure, no negative thoughts or sensations of any kind. His brain is flooded with positive qualia letting him know that his physical, social, and emotional needs are met and that he has nothing to worry about. Is that really any different than what my chickens experience every day? Arguably, my chickens experience little to no negative qualia each day; they can forage inside a huge enclosed area (safe from predators) and have access to all the food and water they need. They can roost high up in the rafters (i.e., their favorite place to be at night), and live in a social grouping that, according to research into chicken social cognition, is exactly the norm for their species (i.e., one rooster, ten hens). My chickens are, like Ricard, living a pleasure-maxed life. He and my chickens have identically pleasure-soaked minds. Which means that any human living a life filled with less pleasure than Ricard (e.g., me, you, a child soldier, everyone else) is technically losing to my chickens at the game of life.

Of course, the way my chickens live is not the norm for the species. And this, too, is a product of human intelligence, and a sad result of the Exceptionalism

Paradox. Humans have the power to create a life of pleasure maximization for chickens. But we typically use that power to create far more misery for them than you would find for an "average" chicken living in the wild. Because humans have devised ways to streamline the production of eggs and meat to maximize our access to food, we have created a situation for farmed chickens that is the stuff of nightmares. Most chickens alive today are stuck in battery cages, deprived of normal roosting, foraging, and socialization. As a whole, chickens likely experience less pleasure than humans. But that is, paradoxically, humans' fault. It's due to human cognition creating more misery for chickens, not more happiness for ourselves.

The future of human intelligence

The human mind is exceptional. We have a capacity that all other species lack: the ability to intentionally produce more pleasure for *other* minds. As why specialists with episodic foresight and theory of mind, we understand that our actions can generate pleasure and misery in the minds of other creatures, be it human or animal. We understand that child soldiers and battery cage hens are miserable. We know these things, and we have the ability to change them. We have the cognitive and technological capacity to create a world that maximizes pleasure for all humans, as well as nonhuman animals. We could flood the world in pleasure qualia, if we wanted to. And this would elevate the value of human intelligence to something beyond that of other species, who cannot conceive of a pleasure-maxed world. If there is one way in which human minds are superior to those of animals in terms of worth, it is our capacity for understanding that pleasure is important and wanting to spread it as far and wide as possible. Paradoxically though, we don't.

One of the reasons I love *Star Trek* is because it envisions a kind of techno-dork utopia like this, where humans live somewhat harmoniously with one another and have eliminated much of the day-to-day suffering that we currently experience. Is *Star Trek*'s pleasure-maximization world a fantasy?

There are two schools of thought on the future of the human species when it comes to creating a pleasure-maxed utopia. In one corner, you have Steven Pinker, the Harvard psychologist and linguist who has written extensively about why there is hope for our species when it comes to bettering ourselves. Pinker points out that humans have been doing a bang-up job of improving our lot in life thanks to the kind of Enlightenment thinking (i.e., "reason applied to human betterment"[32]) that has doubled our average life span in just two hundred years, and reduced global poverty to its current levels (an all-time low). When asked to speculate on the future of our species, Pinker is somewhat optimistic, arguing that "problems are inevitable, but problems are solvable, and solutions create new problems that can be solved in their turn."[33] It's not a promise of an inevitable utopia, but it's got a *Star Trek* ring to it that smacks more of optimism than extinction.

In the other corner you have the philosopher John Gray, who has written many books on humanity's place in the natural world. Gray acknowledges the lovely boost that comes with Enlightenment style–thinking that has given us modern technology and medicine and everything else, but does not seem to have much hope that these advantages will be enough to free humans of the endless cycle of self-destructive prognostic myopia. In his book *Straw Dogs* he writes:

> The growth of knowledge is real and — barring a world-wide catastrophe — it is now irreversible. Improvements in government and society are no less real, but they are temporary. Not only can they be lost, they are sure to be. History is not progress or decline, but recurring gain and loss. The advance of knowledge deludes us into thinking we are different from other animals, but our history shows that we are not.

Yes, it's possible we will break this cycle of inevitable loss and live in a technologically beautiful future like in *Star Trek,* with adamantine cities floating in the sky above lush, untouched rain forests blanketing a rejuvenated Earth. Where biodiversity has been restored, and humans get their food from sustainably grown farming that doesn't require as much land or water usage, and where we have eliminated the animal misery created by current farming practices. That's my daughter's dream for the world. Floating cities. Forests. Life.

She tells me about this as we are on our way to the youth rally for climate change in Halifax. We are driving down the Trans-Canada Highway in my Subaru past new swatches of clear-cut forest dotting the Nova Scotia landscape. We march through the streets in a huge crowd — the largest Halifax has ever seen — demanding that the world's governments take action to address climate change. On the way home, we stop for a coffee and a doughnut and talk about all the ways in which humans are destroying the Earth, and what we need to do to fix it.

A fossil fuel–burning car? Imported coffee? Clear-cutting? A climate rally? That's a whole lot of mixed messages for just one day. I am rotten with prognostic myopia. We are all rotten with prognostic myopia.

I am hopeful that we will find a solution to the existential threats marching toward us. I believe that we can create laws that bypass our decision-making blind spots and channel our collective actions into stopping the threats of climate change and ecological collapse. I hope that the *Star Trek* utopia that is within us becomes a reality. I'm just not sure when that hope bleeds into delusion.

If Nietzsche Were a Narwhal

Let's revisit our old pal Nietzsche. Here's what he had to say about animal happiness:

> Consider the cattle, grazing as they pass you by: they do not know what is meant by yesterday or today, they leap about, eat, rest, digest, leap about again, and so from morn till night and from day to day, fettered to the moment and its pleasure or displeasure, and thus neither melancholy nor bored. This is a hard sight for man to see; for, though he thinks himself better than the animals because he is human, he cannot help envying them their happiness.[34]

The thing is, Nietzsche was wrong about cows. They are not "fettered to the moment." Cows, like most animals, make plans, albeit for the near future. And they experience melancholy. They have a minimal concept of death, and feel some kind of sadness at the loss of their friends and family.

But he was right to acknowledge their capacity for pleasure. He was right to envy their happiness. Depending on the individual cow in question, it's likely that a cow will experience more pleasure in its lifetime than did the soul-tortured Nietzsche. Unlike a Buddhist who seeks to end suffering through the elimination of desire, Nietzsche embraced suffering as a path to meaning. Misery was, for him, a worthy teacher. His human cognitive capacities — his death wisdom, causal inferential skills, and cognitive-linguistic aptitude — brought him no happiness. No pleasure. Only the suffering that he craved. In the end, Nietzsche would have been better off as a narwhal. And, if we think seriously about increasing pleasure and reducing misery on a global scale — the utilitarian utopia — then the world would have been better off if we were all narwhals. Think of the happiness it would spread throughout the animal kingdom if humans suddenly stopped doing all the destructive things that make us human.

Human intelligence is not the miracle of evolution we like to think it is. We love our little accomplishments — our moon landings and megacities — like a parent loves their newborn baby. But nobody loves a baby as much as the parents. The planet does not love us as much as we love our intellect. Because we are indeed exceptional if not necessarily "good," we have generated more death and destruction for life on this planet than any other animal, past and present. Our many intellectual accomplishments are currently on track to produce our own extinction, which is exactly how evolution gets rid of adaptations that suck. It is the greatest of paradoxes that we should have an exceptional mind that seems hell-bent on destroying itself. Unless we can pull out a Pinkerian *Star Trek* solution in the nick of time, human intelligence is going to wink out of existence.

So instead of looking at the cows and chickens and narwhals in your life with pity because they lack human cognitive capacities, think first about the value of those capacities. Do you experience more pleasure than your pets because of them? Is the world a better place thanks to our species' intelligence? If we are honest about the answers to those questions, then there's good reason to tone down our smugness. Because, depending on where we go from here, human intelligence may just be the stupidest thing that has ever happened.

Epilogue

Why save a slug?

My front garden is overrun with slugs in late spring. Their glossy slime trails blanket our driveway, and a few dozen of them take shelter near my car each morning. My daily ritual now involves a slug check, moving them out from under my tires. I cannot imagine simply wantonly driving over a slug. To me, that feels like the behavior of a sociopath.

This has always been my lot in life. I grew up in a home where my mother was a friend to all animals. When I was a small boy, I remember her breaking up a crowd of people who were threatening to step on a bat that was floundering on the sidewalk in front of the drugstore. My mother, who could have been awarded the Nobel Prize for timidity, yelled at everyone to get back. She found a cardboard box, scooped it up, and rescued it.

Whether I inherited my mother's animal empathy mindset or learned by watching her interact with animals is immaterial. I, too, am consumed by a crippling empathy for the living creatures around me. My daughter has been late for school on more than one occasion due to my insistence on morning slug checks. And I don't tolerate squishing bugs, which has resulted in many awkward (and sometimes confrontational) conversations with arachnophobes and fly-bashers over the years.

My academic interest in animal cognition was a logical extension of my upbringing. But it was also constrained by the values and norms I learned during those years. I have only ever conducted observational — not experimental — research on animals. I've never collected data from captive animals. Something deep inside me finds the idea of captivity problematic. Intellectually, I can produce numerous arguments as to why captivity is sometimes necessary and even good for some species. Some captive facilities are doing good work, thanks to their stellar research output and focus on animal welfare with an eye toward conservation. Other facilities, where entertainment overshadows welfare, are just gross. But either way, I feel weird about it. My colleagues have known this about me since my career began, and it has not prevented me from conducting research on dolphins in the wild, or (I hope) contributing something useful to the field.

I do, however, make an exception for mosquitoes, which I do kill. To me, violence is justified in the interest of self-preservation. And this is where the hypocrisy of one's convictions steps into the light. If I were a utili-

tarian, who believed in maximizing pleasure for all creatures, then not only should I not kill mosquitoes, but
actually allow them to drink my blood. My body could
probably withstand many thousands of bites before it
became a serious problem, and it would bring pleasure
to thousands of little mosquito minds. But this seems
absurd to me. And I don't want to do it.

We all have individual ideas about how animals should
be treated. But most of our ideas are not particularly
well considered or derived from some complex ethical
calculation. Most of us learn to treat animals from the
culture around us, be it societal or familial. We live by
unexamined norms. In most of Canada, for example, we
eat pigs but not dogs. But there is no law barring the
practice. In fact, if you raise dogs specifically to eat
them, you are free to turn them into sausages or soup or
whatever. Nonetheless, there is no widespread dog eating in Canada. It's just a norm we abide by.

When I was conducting research in Japan, a colleague
of mine asked if I wanted to try a burger made from
whale meat. I declined. After a protracted discussion
about why I won't eat whale, I asked him if he would
consider eating a burger made from dog meat. He
wouldn't. The Japanese consider dogs pets, not food. It
was an absurd idea to him. I explained that the cultural
taboo for eating dog meat in Japan was the same taboo
many North Americans feel when it comes to whale
meat. I didn't need to invoke any arguments about whale
intelligence or population levels or cruel fishing practices

or any of that. Because the reason most non-Indigenous North American people like me don't eat whale is because they have no (recent) cultural history of eating whale. It's a cultural taboo. The ethical arguments often follow from this taboo like a slime trail following a slug.

It's all so terribly arbitrary. My own convictions don't make much sense on paper. For example, I am not a vegetarian. Despite spending so much of my time caring for my chickens and trying to maximize their health and happiness, I would still eat a chicken burger. I justify it because the chicken has already been turned into a patty. It's simply too late to worry about their happiness levels. Of course, I would never eat one of my own chickens if it should die; we give them a funeral and a proper burial. Crazy, right? I have no uniformly consistent moral framework that outlines my relationship to animals across the board. At times, my convictions are in direct conflict, and seemingly hypocritical.

And I am not alone in being logically inconsistent. In the United States, mice, rats, and birds bred for research are not considered animals according to the Animal Welfare Act, which is how research labs can sidestep welfare rules concerning their treatment.[1] As many as 95 percent of animals used in laboratory research in the US are exempt from federal law that would otherwise ensure their welfare. That's a loophole based not on ethical arguments about animal suffering, but legal arguments concerning the value of these animals to medical science and/or financial stakeholders.

Science gets embroiled in ethical discussions once we go looking for facts about the nature of animal minds to help us determine the extent to which animals suffer. This book is filled with fun facts about animal minds that I hope introduce you to new ways of thinking about the animal kingdom. But if you were hoping to read something that showed once and for all that it's either okay or not okay to, for example, drive over slugs, then you are sure to be disappointed. The science of animal minds cannot, on its own, tell you anything about the morality of your behavior.

I hope I have convincingly argued that all animals have consciousness: subjective experience that helps them make decisions and generate behavior. Animals understand something about the passage of time and make plans for the future — often just moments ahead, but sometimes a few days down the road. Animals understand something about death. They learn how the world works by accumulating associative information about *what* happens *when*, although probably not *why*. Animals do not produce behavior through inflexible instinct, but by a combination of in-built propensities and expectations modified by exposure to the environment and learned information. Animals can be deceptive. Animals have intentions and goals. Animals have norms that guide their social behavior, giving them ideas about what's fair and how they (and others) deserve to be treated. All these cognitive skills have helped nonhuman animals thrive for millions of years. The additional cognitive sprinkles that help humans do what we do (e.g., language, theory of mind, causal inference, death wisdom, etc.) are relatively new additions, and have yet to prove themselves all that valuable to the great arbiter of usefulness: natural selection.

Knowing what we know of animal cognition, am I that crazy for saving the slugs in my driveway each morning? This comes down to two questions, both of which are meaningful to me. First is, how do slugs experience the world? The second is, what does that tell us about how we should be treating them?

Slugs experience the world in ways that give them desires and goals, as well as conscious sensations of pleasure, pain, contentment, etc. I save slugs because it just seems sad to me to take away those things. To be indifferent to a mind that has miraculously sprung into existence after billions of years of nonexistence. What a miracle to exist here and now and have the capacity to experience this world. I want to do my part to make sure I am not the reason a slug's life prematurely ends.

I hope this book will help readers entertain the idea that animals have little qualia-filled minds that are worth taking into consideration. And that your mind is not quite the end all and be all of awesomeness, as if our perceived intellectual superiority justifies indifference to animal suffering.

Is the maximization of pleasure the ultimate goal of life? I think so. Or maybe maximizing the amount of love. I know, bringing up the L-word is uncomfortable when you're trying to think like a scientist. But don't judge its appearance in a book about animal cognition too harshly. Love is just pleasure writ with a fancier pen. Its biological value is obvious. I love my chickens, and they might love me in return, and that makes all of us not just happier, but healthier. It's the happy and healthy animals that pop out the best babies, and that's all that evolution cares about. Evolution values love because *we* value love, even if the universe has no real use for it. "Whatever is done for love always occurs beyond good and evil," wrote Nietzsche.[2] Now that's a sentiment I can get behind, my friend.

Acknowledgments

Writing a book can be a strangely emotional process — full of self-doubt, indecision, crippling realizations, and semi-delusional epiphanies. It's the people around you who guide you toward the finish line with your sanity intact, and a fresh cup of coffee in your hands. So let me present to you those people.

My primary sanity-wrangler has always been — and always will be — my wife, Ranke de Vries. Not only is she usually the one making the coffee, but she also provides feedback on every draft of the book that I send her way. And listens to my armchair monologues as I work my way through ideas. It must be tedious and yet she does it without fail and without grumbling. I cannot be more grateful. Thanks also to my daughter, Mila, who, while far less likely to want to listen to my monologues, makes me laugh every day.

This whole book thing happened in the first place because of my agent, Lisa DiMona. Everyone needs a Lisa in their life. She is my advocate and sounding board,

Acknowledgments

and I am beyond lucky to be in her orbit. To this day, whenever I see an email come into my inbox from Lisa, I get a flutter in my chest.

And then there's Pronoy Sarkar. If I could put anyone's name next to mine on the front cover, it would be Pronoy's. He is not just my editor, but the co-parent of this book baby. Not only has he been a champion of the book and a catalyst for the entire project, but he has been an expert guide when it came to structuring the book and my arguments. What a joy and a privilege to know that Pronoy is in my corner.

Thanks also to the entire team at Little, Brown including Fanta Diallo, Bruce Nichols, Linda Arends, Maria Espinosa, Stacy Schuck, Katherine Akey, Juliana Horbachevsky, Lucy Kim, Melissa Mathlin, and my copy editor, Scott Wilson. Thanks to the many early readers and blurbers (especially Jonathan Balcombe and Barbara J. King), who provided not just kind words, but spotted a few embarrassing problems that I corrected in the final draft.

Thanks to the many experts I interviewed and spoke with for the book, some of whom never made it into the final version, including Jody Green, Dan Ahern, Susana Monsó, Sergey Budaev, Mikael Haller, Mike McCaskill, Lauren Stanton, and Evan Westra. Thanks also to Marie-Luise Theuerkauf for checking the German translation of Nietzsche's writings, and Marianna Di Paolo for the Shoshoni translation.

Several friends appeared as characters in the book

whom I need to thank for allowing me to make them famous and/or infamous, including Andrea Boyd (and her dogs Lucy and Clover), Monica Schuegraf, Michael Cardinal-Aucoin, and Brendan Ahern. Thanks also to my academic friends willing to chat with me about my ideas for the book including Russell Wyeth, Clare Fawcett, Christie Lomore, and Doug Al-Maini. A special thanks to the members of my writing group who were so supportive of my initial book ideas, including John Graham-Pole (and Dorothy Lander too!), Peter Smith, and Anne Louise MacDonald. Angus MacCaull is not just my writing group pal, but a champion of my writing career and I am grateful to him for the many years of advice and advocacy.

Thanks to the many artsy co-conspirators and friends in my life who have been so encouraging of my writing ambitions these past couple of years including Laura Teasdale (my improv and music muse), the Ritchie clan (Julia, Peter, and Harriet), Dave Lawrence (my podcasting muse and one of the first people to read the book in its entirety), Jenn Priddle (my vault and cheerleader), Erin Cole, Michael Linkletter, Steve Stamatopoulos, Ashley Shepphard, Natasha MacKinnon, Rob Hull, Allan Briggs, Ayami Uemura, Brendan Lucey, James Brinck, Jenn MacDonald, and oh my gosh I just realized I have too many people to thank, so a big *thank-you* to everyone I know and love!

Thanks to all my D&D pals for the hundreds (thousands?) of hours of shenanigans that brought such joy and laughter and distraction from my book woes, including Jake Hanlon, Paul Tynan, Wojtek Tokarz, Jon

Acknowledgments

Langdon, Sarah O'Toole, Donovan Purcell, Robin MacDougall, Ben Lane-Smith, and Grace Lane-Smith. Thanks to my dad-band pals who also make an appearance in the book: Julien Landry, Ryan Lukeman, Cory Bishop, and Adrian Cameron. Thanks to my Netflix support group Donna Trembinski, Michael Spearin, Susan Hawkes, and Cory Rushton. Thanks also to the many colleagues and friends at StFX, and a very special thank-you to my longtime friends and partners at the Dolphin Communication Project: Kathleen Dudzinski, Kelly Melillo-Sweeting, and John Anderson; you have been such amazing colleagues over the years and so much of my success is thanks to our collaboration.

A big thanks to Mijke and Marcel van den Berg and Thijmen, Pepijn, and Madelief for joining us on this Canadian adventure! And to my family back home in New England and the Netherlands, and the many people and pals across the globe with whom I have shared laughs over the years.

And a very special thanks to all the animals in my life. Without the connection I have had with the many animals I have known, both wild and domestic, this book would never have existed. From the crows that greet me each morning on my deck, to Oscar (who also makes an appearance in this book), as well as the chickens that bring us such joy (Echo, Dr. Becky, Ghost, Specter, Topaz, Shadow, Mist, Coffee, Brownie, Muffin, Mocha, Song, and Dragon). And of course to the OG animal pal in my life, Tigger.

Thanks everyone, and stay tuned for the next book!

Notes

Introduction

1. Nietzsche, F. W. (1964). *Thoughts out of season, part II* (see "Schopenhauer as Educator"). Trans. A. Collins. Russell and Russell.
2. "The deeper minds of all ages have had pity for animals, because they have not the power to turn the sting of the suffering against themselves, and understand their being metaphysically." From Nietzsche, F. W. (2011). *Thoughts out of season, part II.* Project Gutenberg.
3. Nicholsen, S. W. (1997). *Untimely meditations,* trans. R. J. Hollingdale.
4. Hemelsoet, D., Hemelsoet, K., & Devreese, D. (2008). The neurological illness of Friedrich Nietzsche. *Acta neurologica belgica, 108*(1), 9.
5. *Ecce Homo, Twilight of the Idols,* and *The Antichrist.*
6. Young, J. (2010). *Friedrich Nietzsche: A philosophical biography.* Cambridge University Press, 531.
7. Diethe, C. (2003). *Nietzsche's sister and the will to power: A biography of Elisabeth Förster-Nietzsche* (Vol. 22). University of Illinois Press.
8. There is some speculation that the Turin horse events might be apocryphal.
9. Hemelsoet, D., Hemelsoet, K., & Devreese, D. (2008). The neurological illness of Friedrich Nietzsche. *Acta neurologica belgica, 108*(1), 9.

Notes

10. Monett, D. and Lewis, C. W. P. (2018). Getting clarity by defining Artificial Intelligence — A Survey. In Muller, V. C., ed., *Philosophy and Theory of Artificial Intelligence* 2017, volume SAPERE 44. Springer. 212–214.

11. Wang, P. (2008). What do you mean by "AI"? In Wang, P., Goertzel, B., and Franklin, S., eds., *Artificial General Intelligence* 2008. Proceedings of the First AGI Conference, Frontiers in Artificial Intelligence and Applications, volume 171. IOS Press. 362–373.

12. Monett, D., Lewis, C. W., & Thórisson, K. R. (2020). Introduction to the JAGI Special Issue "On Defining Artificial Intelligence" — Commentaries and Author's Response. *Journal of Artificial General Intelligence, 11*(2), 1–100.

13. Spearman, C. (1904). "General Intelligence," objectively determined and measured. *American Journal of Psychology, 15*(2): 201–293. doi:10.2307/1412107

14. aip.org/history-programs/niels-bohr-library/oral-histories/30591-1

15. Lattman, P. (2007, September 27). The origins of Justice Stewart's "I know it when I see it." *Wall Street Journal*. LawBlog. Retrieved December 31, 2014.

16. Diethe, C. (2003). *Nietzsche's sister and the will to power: A biography of Elisabeth Förster-Nietzsche* (Vol. 22). University of Illinois Press.

17. Salmi, H. (1994). Die Sucht nach dem germanischen Ideal. Bernhard Förster (1843–1889) als Wegbereiter des Wagnerismus. *Zeitschrift für Geschichtswissenschaft, 6*, 485–496.

18. Ellison, K. (1998, September 10). Racial purity dies in the jungle vision: Founders saw their Paraguayan settlement as a place that would spawn a race of Aryan supermen. But they didn't take into account disease, heat and inbreeding. *The Baltimore Sun*. Retrieved from baltimoresun.com/news/bs-xpm-1998-09-10-1998253112-story.html

19. Leiter, B. (2015, December 21). Nietzsche's Hatred of "Jew Hatred." Review of *Nietzsche's Jewish problem: Between anti-Semitism and anti-Judaism* by Robert C. Holub. *The New Rambler*.

20. Nietzsche, F. W. (1901). *Der wille zur macht: versuch einer umwerthung aller werthe (studien und fragmente)*. Vol. 15. CG Naumann.
21. Macintyre, B. (2013). *Forgotten fatherland: The search for Elisabeth Nietzsche*. A&C Black.
22. Santaniello, W. (2012). *Nietzsche, God, and the Jews: His critique of Judeo-Christianity in relation to the Nazi myth*. SUNY Press.
23. Golomb, J., & Wistrich, R. S. (Eds.). (2009). *Nietzsche, godfather of fascism?: On the uses and abuses of a philosophy*. Princeton University Press.
24. Southwell, G. (2009). *A beginner's guide to Nietzsche's Beyond Good and Evil*. John Wiley & Sons.
25. Nietzsche, F. W. (2018). *The twilight of the idols*. Jovian Press.
26. My neighbor and Nietzsche scholar Dan Ahern describes him as a "nice, gentle, well-mannered guy — not a misanthrope as you would expect."
27. United States Holocaust Memorial and Museum. (2019, February 4). Documenting numbers of victims of the Holocaust and Nazi persecution.

Chapter 1

1. Nietzsche, F. W. (1887). *Die fröhliche Wissenschaft: ("La gaya scienza")*. E. W. Fritzsch. Translated from this passage: "Der Mensch ist allmählich zu einem phantastischen Tiere geworden, welches eine Existenz-Bedingung mehr als jedes andre Tier zu erfüllen hat: der Mensch muß von Zeit zu Zeit glauben, zu wissen, warum er existiert."
2. Thanks to David Hill for profiling Mike in the Ringer: Hill, D. (2021, February 16). The beach bum who beat Wall Street and made millions on GameStop. The Ringer. theringer.com/2021/2/16/22284786/gamestop-stock-wall-street-short-squeeze-beach-volleyball-referee
3. Gilbert, B. (2020, January 23). The world's biggest video game retailer, GameStop, is dying: Here's what led to the retail giant's slow demise. *Business Insider*. businessinsider.com/gamestop

Notes

-worlds-biggest-video-game-retailer-decline-explained -2019-7

4. markets.businessinsider.com/news/stocks/gamestop-stock-price -retail-traders-shorts-citron-andrew-left-gme-2021-1-102 9994276

5. King, M. (2013, January 13). Investments: Orlando is the cat's whiskers of stock picking. *The Guardian*. theguardian.com/ money/2013/jan/13/investments-stock-picking

6. Video game Michael Pachter analyst weighs in on GameStop's earnings call. (2021, March 26) CNBC. youtube.com/watch? v=fOJV_qaJ2ew

7. McBrearty, S., & Jablonski, N. G. (2005). First fossil chimpanzee. *Nature, 437*(7055), 105–108.

8. Karmin, M., et al. (2015). A recent bottleneck of Y chromosome diversity coincides with a global change in culture. *Genome Research, 25*(4), 459–466.

9. The exact shape (although not size) of the human brain would settle into place between 100,000 and 35,000 years ago, but these Baringo relatives of ours were arguably quite similar to modern humans cognitively. See Neubauer, S., Hublin, J. J., & Gunz, P. (2018). The evolution of modern human brain shape. *Science Advances, 4*(1), eaao5961.

10. Zihlman, A. L., & Bolter, D. R. (2015). Body composition in Pan paniscus compared with Homo sapiens has implications for changes during human evolution. *Proceedings of the National Academy of Sciences, 112*(24), 7466–7471.

11. bbc.com/earth/story/20160204-why-do-humans-have-chins

12. Brown, K. S., et al. (2009). Fire as an engineering tool of early modern humans. *Science, 325*(5942), 859–862.

13. Aubert, M., et al. (2019). Earliest hunting scene in prehistoric art. *Nature, 576*(7787), 442–445.

14. Culotta, Elizabeth. (2009). On the origin of religion. *Science, 326*(5954). 784–787. 10.1126/science.326_784

15. Snir, A., et al. (2015).The Origin of Cultivation and Proto-Weeds, Long Before Neolithic Farming. *PLOS ONE, 10*(7): e0131422 DOI: 10.1371/journal.pone.0131422

16. *Burrowing bettong.* (n.d.). Australian Wildlife Conservancy. australianwildlife.org/wildlife/burrowing-bettong/

Notes

17. Tay, N. E., Fleming, P. A., Warburton, N. M., & Moseby, K. E. (2021). Predator exposure enhances the escape behaviour of a small marsupial, the burrowing bettong. *Animal Behaviour, 175*, 45–56.

18. Visalberghi, E., & Tomasello, M. (1998). Primate causal understanding in the physical and psychological domains. *Behavioural Processes, 42*(2-3), 189–203.

19. Suddendorf, T. (2013). *The gap: The science of what separates us from other animals.* Constellation.

20. Millikan, R. (2006). Styles of rationality. In S. Hurley & M. Nudds (Eds.). *Rational animals?, 117–126.*

21. Jacobs, I. F., & Osvath, M. (2015). The string-pulling paradigm in comparative psychology. *Journal of Comparative Psychology, 129*(2), 89.

22. Heinrich, B. (1995). An experimental investigation of insight in common ravens (Corvus corax). *The Auk, 112*(4), 994–1003.

23. Taylor, A. H., et al. (2010). An investigation into the cognition behind spontaneous string pulling in New Caledonian crows. *PloS one, 5*(2), e9345.

24. Völter, C. J., & Call, J. (2017). Causal and inferential reasoning in animals. In G. M Burghardt, I. M. Pepperberg, C. T. Snowdon, & T. Zentall (Eds). *APA handbook of comparative psychology Vol. 2: Perception, learning, and cognition.* American Psychological Association, 643–671.

25. Owuor, B. O., & Kisangau, D. P. (2006). Kenyan medicinal plants used as antivenin: a comparison of plant usage. *Journal of Ethnobiology and Ethnomedicine, 2*(1), 7.

26. Luft, D. (2020). Medieval Welsh medical texts. Volume one: the recipes. University of Wales Press, 96 (Welsh text on 97).

27. Harrison, F., et al.. (2015). A 1,000-year-old antimicrobial remedy with antistaphylococcal activity. MBio, 6(4).

28. Mann, W. N. (1983). G. E. R. Lloyd (ed.). Hippocratic writings. Translated by J. Chadwick. Penguin, 262.

29. The mechanics of how this works is not exactly clear. Snake venom was considered by Avicenna and the other humorism experts to be hot. Chicken butts were also considered by Avicenna to be hot, potentially because those butts produced feces — and all dung and feces were considered hot. So maybe

the dung-smothered chicken butt attracted the venom because they were both hot? My wife is an expert on these things and advised me not to speculate lest I run afoul of the medievalists. There's plenty to read about this subject in the following articles: Walker-Meikle, K. (2014). Toxicology and treatment: medical authorities and snake-bite in the middle ages. *Korot, 22*: 85–104. Vries, R. de (2019). A short tract on medicinal uses for animal dung. *North American Journal of Celtic Studies, 3*(2), 111–136.

30. Collier, R. (2009). Legumes, lemons and streptomycin: A short history of the clinical trial. *Canadian Medical Association Journal, 180*(1): 23–24.

31. Schloegl, C., & Fischer, J. (2017). Causal reasoning in nonhuman animals. *The Oxford Handbook of Causal Reasoning,* 699–715.

32. Huffman, M. A. (1997). Current evidence for self-medication in primates: A multidisciplinary perspective. *American Journal of Physical Anthropology: The Official Publication of the American Association of Physical Anthropologists, 104*(S25), 171–200.

33. pnas.org/content/111/49/17339

34. Levenson, R. M., Krupinski, E. A., Navarro, V. M., & Wasserman, E. A. (2015). Pigeons (Columba livia) as trainable observers of pathology and radiology breast cancer images. *PloS one, 10*(11), e0141357.

35. Morton, S. G., & Combe, G. (1839). *Crania Americana; or, a comparative view of the skulls of various aboriginal nations of North and South America: to which is prefixed an essay on the varieties of the human species.* Philadelphia: J. Dobson; London: Simpkin, Marshall.

36. Cotton-Barratt, O., et al. (2016). Global catastrophic risks. A report of the Global Challenges Foundation/Global Priorities Project.

Chapter 2

1. Nietzsche, F. W. (2015). *Über Wahrheit und Lüge im außermoralischen Sinn: ("Was bedeutet das alles?").* Reclam Verlag. Translated from this passage: "Was ist also Wahrheit? Ein bewegliches Heer von Metaphern, Metonymien, Anthropomorphismen, kurz eine Summe von menschlichen Relationen, die, poetisch und

rhetorisch gesteigert, übertragen, geschmückt wurden und die nach langem Gebrauch einem Volke fest, kanonisch und verbindlich dünken: die Wahrheiten sind Illusionen, von denen man vergessen hat, daß sie welche sind."

2. Bogus Lancashire vet jailed after botched castration. (2010, January 11). BBC News. news.bbc.co.uk/2/hi/uk_news/england/merseyside/8453020.stm

3. Tozer, J, & Hull, L. (2010, January 12). Bogus doctor and vet who conned patients out of more than £50,000 jailed for 2 years. *The Daily Mail.* dailymail.co.uk/news/article-1242375/Bogus-doctor-conned-patients-50-000-pay-child-maintenance-jailed.html

4. The man who exposed bogus GP Russell Oakes speaks. (2010, January 12). *Liverpool Echo.* liverpoolecho.co.uk/news/liverpool-news/man-who-exposed-bogus-gp-3433329

5. Equine osteopath used forged degree to register as a vet. (2008, March 20). *Horse & Hound.* horseandhound.co.uk/news/equine-osteopath-used-forged-degree-to-register-as-a-vet-199362

6. The man who exposed bogus GP Russell Oakes speaks. (2010, January 12). *Liverpool Echo.* liverpoolecho.co.uk/news/liverpool-news/man-who-exposed-bogus-gp-3433329

7. Bogus Lancashire vet jailed after botched castration. (2010, January 11). BBC News. http://news.bbc.co.uk/2/hi/uk_news/england/merseyside/8453020.stm

8. How bogus GP Russell Oakes made others in Merseyside believe his lies. (2010, January 12). *Liverpool Echo.* liverpoolecho.co.uk/news/liverpool-news/how-bogus-gp-russell-oakes-3433327

9. Fraudulent vet: The bigger picture (2010, June) RCVS News. The Newsletter of the Royal College of Veterinary Surgeons.

10. Souchet, J., & Aubret, F. (2016). Revisiting the fear of snakes in children: the role of aposematic signalling. *Scientific reports,* 6(1), 1–7.

11. Merriam-Webster. (n.d.). Aichmophobia. In Merriam-Webster.com dictionary. merriam-webster.com/dictionary/aichmophobia

12. Nietzsche, F. W. (1994). *Nietzsche: "On the genealogy of morality" and other writings.* Cambridge University Press.

13. Gallup, G. G. (1973). Tonic immobility in chickens: Is a stimulus that signals shock more aversive than the receipt of shock? *Animal Learning & Behavior,* 1(3), 228–232.

14. See Byrne, R. W., & Whiten, A. (1985). Tactical deception of familiar individuals in baboons (Papio ursinus). *Animal Behaviour, 33*(2), 669–673. And also: Whiten, A., & Byrne, R. W. (1988). Tactical deception in primates. *Behavioral and brain sciences, 11*(2), 233–244.

15. Brown, C., Garwood, M. P., & Williamson, J. E. (2012). It pays to cheat: tactical deception in a cephalopod social signalling system. *Biology letters, 8*(5), 729–732.

16. Heberlein, M. T., Manser, M. B., & Turner, D. C. (2017). Deceptive-like behaviour in dogs (Canis familiaris). *Animal Cognition, 20*(3), 511–520.

17. *Theory of mind* is a term coined in 1978 by David Premack and Guy Woodruff: Premack, D., & Woodruff, G. (1978). Does the chimpanzee have a theory of mind? *Behavioral and Brain Sciences, 1*(4), 515–526.

18. Krupenye, C., & Call, J. (2019). Theory of mind in animals: Current and future directions. *Wiley Interdisciplinary Reviews: Cognitive Science, 10*(6), e1503.

19. Krupenye, C., et al. (2016). Great apes anticipate that other individuals will act according to false beliefs. *Science, 354*(6308), 110–114.

20. Oesch, N. (2016). Deception as a derived function of language. *Frontiers in Psychology, 7*, 1485.

21. The story of Leo Koretz that I am relaying here can be found in the wonderfully researched book *Empire of Deception* by Dean Jobb (Harper Avenue, 2015).

22. Levine, T. R. (2019). *Duped: Truth-default theory and the social science of lying and deception.* University of Alabama Press.

23. Serota, K. B., Levine, T. R., & Boster, F. J. (2010). The prevalence of lying in America: Three studies of self-reported lies. *Human Communication Research, 36*(1), 2–25.

24. Curtis, D. A., & Hart, C. L. (2020). Pathological lying: Theoretical and empirical support for a diagnostic entity. *Psychiatric Research and Clinical Practice,* appi-prcp.

25. Paige, L. E., Fields, E. C., & Gutchess, A. (2019). Influence of age on the effects of lying on memory. *Brain and Cognition, 133*, 42–53.

26. This is an actual method for interrogating a witness. See: Walczyk, J. J., Igou, F. D., Dixon, L. P., & Tcholakian, T. (2013).

Advancing lie detection by inducing cognitive load on liars: a review of relevant theories and techniques guided by lessons from polygraph-based approaches. *Frontiers in Psychology, 4,* 14.

27. Chandler, M., Fritz, A. S., & Hala, S. (1989). Small-scale deceit: Deception as a marker of two-, three-, and four-year-olds' early theories of mind. *Child Development, 60*(6), 1263–1277.

28. Talwar, V., & Lee, K. (2008). Social and cognitive correlates of children's lying behavior. *Child Development, 79*(4), 866–881.

29. Jensen, L. A., Arnett, J. J., Feldman, S. S., & Cauffman, E. (2004). The right to do wrong: Lying to parents among adolescents and emerging adults. *Journal of Youth and Adolescence, 33*(2), 101–112.

30. Knox, D., Schacht, C., Holt, J., & Turner, J. (1993). Sexual lies among university students. *College Student Journal, 27*(2), 269–272.

31. See definitions in: Petrocelli, J. V. (2018). Antecedents of bullshitting. *Journal of Experimental Social Psychology, 76,* 249–258. And Turpin, M. H., et al. (2021). Bullshit Ability as an Honest Signal of Intelligence. *Evolutionary Psychology, 19*(2), 14747049211000317.

32. *Truthiness* was famously introduced to the world by Stephen Colbert in 2005 on *The Colbert Report,* and was subsequently announced as Merriam-Webster Dictionary's word of the year in 2006. The definition provided here is from the Oxford Dictionaries.

33. Turpin, M. H., et al. (2021). Bullshit ability as an honest signal of intelligence. *Evolutionary Psychology, 19*(2), 14747049211000317.

34. Templer, K. J. (2018). Dark personality, job performance ratings, and the role of political skill: An indication of why toxic people may get ahead at work. *Personality and Individual Differences, 124,* 209–214.

35. Templer, K. (2018). Why do toxic people get promoted? For the same reason humble people do: Political skill. *Harvard Business Review, 10.*

36. cnn.com/2017/10/17/politics/russian-oligarch-putin-chef-troll-factory/index.html

37. Rosenblum, N. L., & Muirhead, R. (2020). *A lot of people are saying: The new conspiracism and the assault on democracy.* Princeton University Press.

38. Department of Justice. (2018). Grand jury indicts thirteen Russian individuals and three Russian companies for scheme to interfere in the United States political system. Department of Justice.

39. Broniatowski, D. A., et al. (2018). Weaponized health communication: Twitter bots and Russian trolls amplify the vaccine debate. *American Journal of Public Health, 108*(10), 1378–1384.

40. Reinhart, R. (2020, January 14). Fewer in US continue to see vaccines as important. *Gallup.*

41. callingbullshit.org/syllabus.html

42. Bergstrom, C. T., & West, J. D. (2020). *Calling bullshit: The art of skepticism in a data-driven world.* Random House.

43. Henley, J. (2020, January 29). How Finland starts its fight against fake news in primary schools. *The Guardian.* theguardian.com/world/2020/jan/28/fact-from-fiction-finlands-new-lessons-in-combating-fake-news

44. Lessenski, M. (2019). Just think about it. Findings of the Media Literacy Index 2019. Open Society Institute Sophia. osis.bg/?p=3356&lang=en

45. For handy methods on bullshit detection, check out Carl Sagan's chapter — "The Fine Art of Baloney Detection" — in his 1995 book, *The Demon-Haunted World,* and social psychologist John Petrocelli's *The Life-Changing Science of Detecting Bullshit.*

Chapter 3

1. Nietzsche, F. W. (1887). *Die fröhliche Wissenschaft: ("La gaya scienza").* E. W. Fritzsch. Translated from this passage: "Wie seltsam, daß diese einzige Sicherheit und Gemeinsamkeit fast gar nichts über die Menschen vermag und daß sie am weitesten davon entfernt sind, sich als die Brüderschaft des Todes zu fühlen!"

2. Selk, A. (August 12, 2018). Update: Orca abandons body of her dead calf after a heartbreaking, weeks-long journey. *The Washington Post.* washingtonpost.com/news/animalia/wp/2018/08/10/the-stunning-devastating-weeks-long-journey-of-an-orca-and-her-dead-calf/

3. Orcas now taking turns floating dead calf in apparent mourning ritual. (2018, July 31). CBC Radio. cbc.ca/radio/asithappens/

Notes

as-it-happens-tuesday-edition-1.4768344/orcas-now
-appear-to-be-taking-turns-floating-dead-calf-in-apparent
-mourning-ritual-1.4768349

4. Mapes, L. W. (2018, August 8). "I am sobbing": Mother orca still carrying her dead calf — 16 days later. *The Seattle Times.* seattle times.com/seattle-news/environment/i-am-sobbing-mother -orca-still-carrying-her-dead-calf-16-days-later/

5. Howard, J. (2018, August 14). The "grieving" orca mother? Projecting emotions on animals is a sad mistake. *The Guardian.* theguard ian.com/commentisfree/2018/aug/14/grieving-orca-mother -emotions-animals-mistake

6. Darwin, C. (1871). *The descent of man.* London, UK: John Murray.

7. King, B. J. (2013). *How animals grieve.* University of Chicago Press.

8. Gonçalves, A., & Biro, D. (2018). Comparative thanatology, an integrative approach: exploring sensory/cognitive aspects of death recognition in vertebrates and invertebrates. *Philosophical Transactions of the Royal Society B: Biological Sciences, 373*(1754), 20170263.

9. Mayer, P. (2013, May 27). Questions for Barbara J. King, author of "How animals grieve." NPR. npr.org/2013/05/27/185815445/ questions-for-barbara-j-king-author-of-how-animals-grieve

10. Monsó, S., & Osuna-Mascaró, A. J. (2021). Death is common, so is understanding it: The concept of death in other species. *Synthese,* 199, 2251–2275.

11. Monsó, S., & Osuna-Mascaró, A. J. (2021). Death is common, so is understanding it: the concept of death in other species. *Synthese,* 199, 2251–2275.

12. Nicholsen, S. W. (1997). *Untimely Meditations,* trans. R. J. Hollingdale.

13. de Winter, N. J., et al. (2020). Subdaily-scale chemical variability in a Torreites sanchezi rudist shell: Implications for rudist paleobiology and the Cretaceous day-night cycle. *Paleoceanography and Paleoclimatology, 35*(2), e2019PA003723.

14. See the following brilliant book for more info on sleep: Walker, M. (2017). *Why we sleep: Unlocking the power of sleep and dreams.* Simon and Schuster.

Notes

15. Suddendorf, T., & Corballis, M. C. (2007). The evolution of foresight: What is mental time travel, and is it unique to humans? *Behavioral and brain sciences, 30*(3), 299–313.

16. Adapted from a definition provided by: Hudson, J. A., Mayhew, E. M., & Prabhakar, J. (2011). The development of episodic foresight: Emerging concepts and methods. *Advances in Child Development and Behavior, 40*, 95–137.

17. Thanks to Marianna Di Paolo, Director of the WRMC Shoshoni Language Project & Center for American Indian Languages with the University of Utah. She was able to confirm the Shoshoni name for this bird, and noted that "the word tookottsi is widely used throughout Shoshone land, and probably dates back over a thousand years."

18. Ogden, L. (2016, November 11). Better know a bird: The Clark's nutcracker and its obsessive seed hoarding. *Audubon*. audubon .org/news/better-know-bird-clarks-nutcracker-and-its -obsessive-seed-hoarding

19. Hutchins, H. E., & Lanner, R. M. (1982). The central role of Clark's nutcracker in the dispersal and establishment of whitebark pine. *Oecologia, 55*(2), 192–201.

20. Balda, R. P., & Kamil, A. C. (1992). Long-term spatial memory in Clark's nutcracker, Nucifraga columbiana. *Animal Behaviour, 44*(4), 761–769.

21. Suddendorf, T., & Redshaw, J. (2017). Anticipation of future events. *Encyclopedia of Animal Cognition and Behavior*, 1–9.

22. McCambridge F. (n.d.). This is why chimpanzees throw their poop at us. The Jane Goodall Institute of Canada. janegoodall. ca/our-stories/why-chimpanzees-throw-poop-at-us/

23. Osvath, M. (2009). Spontaneous planning for future stone throwing by a male chimpanzee. *Current Biology, 19*(5), R190–R191.

24. Osvath, M., & Karvonen, E. (2012). Spontaneous innovation for future deception in a male chimpanzee. *PloS One, 7*(5), e36782.

25. Osvath, M. (2010). Great ape foresight is looking great. *Animal Cognition, 13*(5), 777–781.

26. Biotechnology and Biological Sciences Research Council. (2007, February 26). Birds found to plan for the future. *ScienceDaily*. sciencedaily.com/releases/2007/02/070222160144.htm

27. Raby, C. R., Alexis, D. M., Dickinson, A., & Clayton, N. S. (2007). Planning for the future by western scrub-jays. *Nature, 445*(7130), 919–921.

28. Anderson, J. R., Biro, D., & Pettitt, P. (2018). Evolutionary thanatology. *Philosophical Transactions of the Royal Society B: Biological Sciences, 373*(1754): 20170262.

29. Anderson, J. R. (2018). Chimpanzees and death. *Philosophical Transactions of the Royal Society B: Biological Sciences, 373*(1754), 20170257.

30. Varki, A., & Brower, D. (2013). *Denial: Self-deception, false beliefs, and the origins of the human mind.* Hachette UK.

31. Varki, A. (2009). Human uniqueness and the denial of death. *Nature, 460*(7256), 684.

32. Becker, E. (1997). *The denial of death.* Simon and Schuster.

33. Depression. (2021, 13 September). The World Health Organization. who.int/news-room/fact-sheets/detail/depression

Chapter 4

1. Nietzsche, F. W. (1881). *Morgenröthe.* Translated from this passage: "Wir halten die Tiere nicht für moralische Wesen. Aber meint ihr denn, daß die Tiere uns für moralische Wesen halten? — Ein Tier, welches reden konnte, sagte: »Menschlichkeit ist ein Vorurteil, an dem wenigstens wir Tiere nicht leiden."

2. For a description of the Sakai incident, read Bargen, D. G. (2006). *Suicidal honor: General Nogi and the writings of Mori Ogai and Natsume Soseki.* University of Hawaii Press.

3. De Waal, F. (2013) *The bonobo and the atheist: In search of humanism among the primates.* W. W. Norton.

4. A description of this behavior can be found in de Waal, F. B. M., & R. Ren (1988). Comparison of the reconciliation behavior of stumptail and rhesus macaques. *Ethology,* 78: 129–142.

5. I first saw this definition in a presentation by Westra during the June 2021 online conference organized by Andrews and Westra called Normative Animals Online Conference. It will be appearing in a forthcoming journal article by Andrews and Westra titled "A New Framework for the Psychology of Norms."

6. Some philosophers and animal behavior scientists do use the

Notes

term "moral" to describe animals that rely on these more sophisticated feelings/emotions to arrive at behavioral norms. In the book *Wild Justice,* cognitive ethologist Marc Bekoff and philosopher Jessica Pierce cite altruism, tolerance, forgiveness, and fairness as feelings that guide animals' normative behavior, which they argue are complex enough to be elevated to the level of morality. Bekoff, M., & Pierce, J. (2009). *Wild justice: The moral lives of animals.* University of Chicago Press. The philosopher Mark Rowlands argues in his book *Can Animals Be Moral* that "animals can act morally in the sense that they can act on the basis of moral emotions." These moral emotions include the sense of fairness Brosnan and de Waal described for macaques, as well as "sympathy and compassion, kindness, tolerance, and patience, and also their negative counterparts such as anger, indignation, malice, and spite." Rowlands, M. (2015). *Can animals be moral?* Oxford University Press.

7. Hsu, M., Anen, C., & Quartz, S. R. (2008). The right and the good: distributive justice and neural encoding of equity and efficiency. *Science, 320*(5879), 1092–1095.

8. Reingberg, S. (2008). Fairness is a hard-wired emotion. ABC News. abcnews.go.com/Health/Healthday/story?id=4817130&page=1

9. De Waal, F. (2013). *The bonobo and the atheist: In search of humanism among the primates.* W. W. Norton.

10. Old Testament (Leviticus 11:27).

11. Tomasello, M. (2016). *A natural history of human morality.* Harvard University Press.

12. Boesch, C. (2005). Joint cooperative hunting among wild chimpanzees: Taking natural observations seriously. *Behavioral and Brain Sciences, 28*(5), 692–693.

13. Truth and Reconciliation Commission of Canada. (2015). *Honouring the truth, reconciling for the future: Summary of the final report of the Truth and Reconciliation Commission of Canada.* Canada: McGill-Queen's University Press.

14. Truth and Reconciliation Commission of Canada. (2015). *Honouring the truth, reconciling for the future: Summary of the final report of the Truth and Reconciliation Commission of Canada.* Canada: McGill-Queen's University Press.

15. Graham, E. (1997). *The mush hole: Life at two Indian residential schools*. Heffle Pub.

16. cbc.ca/news/canada/toronto/mississauga-pastor-catholic-church -residential-schools-1.6077248

17. Wolfe, R. (1980). Putative threat to national security as a Nuremberg defense for genocide. *The Annals of the American Academy of Political and Social Science, 450*(1), 46–67.

18. Rheault, D. (2011). Solving the "Indian problem": Assimilation laws, practices & Indian residential schools. *Ontario Metis Family Records Center.*

19. Wrangham, R. W., & Peterson, D. (1996). *Demonic males: Apes and the origins of human violence*. Houghton Mifflin Harcourt.

20. Hrdy, S. B. (2011). *Mothers and others*. Harvard University Press.

21. Associated Press. (1968, February 8). Major describes moves. Associated Press.

22. Hrdy, S. B. (2011). *Mothers and others*. Harvard University Press.

23. Young, L. C., Zaun, B. J., & VanderWerf, E. A. (2008). Successful same-sex pairing in Laysan albatross. *Biology Letters, 4*(4), 323–325.

24. Resko, J. A., et al. (1996). Endocrine correlates of partner preference behavior in rams. *Biology of Reproduction, 55*(1), 120–126.

25. Leupp, Gary P. *Male colors*. University of California Press, 1995.

26. economist.com/open-future/2018/06/06/how-homosexuality -became-a-crime-in-the-middle-east

27. Glassgold, J. M., et al. (2009). Report of the American Psychological Association Task Force on appropriate therapeutic responses to sexual orientation. *American Psychological Association.*

28. Flores, A. R., Langton, L., Meyer, I. H., & Romero, A. P. (2020). Victimization rates and traits of sexual and gender minorities in the United States: Results from the National Crime Victimization Survey, 2017. *Science Advances, 6*(40), eaba6910.

29. Translated from wciom.ru/analytical-reviews/analiticheskii-obzor/ teoriya-zagovora-protiv-rossii-

30. nbcnews.com/feature/nbc-out/1-5-russians-want-gays-lesbians -eliminated-survey-finds-n1191851

31. Graham, R., et al. (2011). The health of lesbian, gay, bisexual, and transgender people: Building a foundation for better understanding. Washington, DC: Institute of Medicine.
32. Gates, G. J. (2011). How many people are lesbian, gay, bisexual and transgender? The Williams Institute.

Chapter 5

1. Nietzsche, F. W. (1977). *Nachgelassene Fragmente: Juli 1882 bis Winter 1883-1884*. Walter de Gruyter. Translated from this passage: "Was kümmert mich das Schnurren dessen, der nicht lieben kann, gleich der Katze."
2. Nagel, T. (1974). What is it like to be a bat? *Philosophical Review, 83*, 435–450.
3. Dennett, D. C. (1988). Quining Qualia. In: Marcel, A., & Bisiach, E. (eds.) *Consciousness in Modern Science*, Oxford University Press.
4. van Giesen, L., Kilian, P. B., Allard, C. A., & Bellono, N. W. (2020). Molecular basis of chemotactile sensation in octopus. *Cell, 183*(3), 594–604.
5. The Cambridge Declaration on Consciousness (Archive). (2012, July 7). Written by Low, P., and edited by Panksepp, J., Reiss, D., Edelman, D., Van Swinderen, B., Low, P., and Koch, C. University of Cambridge.
6. Siegel, R. K., & Brodie, M. (1984). Alcohol self-administration by elephants. *Bulletin of the Psychonomic Society, 22*(1), 49–52.
7. Bastos, A. P., et al. (2021). Self-care tooling innovation in a disabled kea (Nestor notabilis). *Scientific Reports, 11*(1), 1–8.
8. Corlett, E. (2021, September 10). "He has adapted": Bruce the disabled New Zealand parrot uses tools for preening. *The Guardian*. theguardian.com/environment/2021/sep/10/the-disabled-new-zealand-parrot-kea-using-tools-for-preening-aoe
9. Edelman, D. B., & Seth, A. K. (2009). Animal consciousness: a synthetic approach. *Trends in Neurosciences, 32*(9), 476–484.
10. Chittka, L., & Wilson, C. (2019). Expanding consciousness. *American Scientist, 107*, 364–369.
11. Queen Mary, University of London. (2009, November 18). Big-

ger not necessarily better, when it comes to brains. ScienceDaily. sciencedaily.com/releases/2009/11/091117124009.htm

12. Barron, A. B., & Klein, C. (2016). What insects can tell us about the origins of consciousness. *Proceedings of the National Academy of Sciences, 113*(18), 4900–4908.

13. Loukola, O. J., Perry, C. J., Coscos, L., & Chittka, L. (2017). Bumblebees show cognitive flexibility by improving on an observed complex behavior. *Science, 355*(6327), 833–836.

14. Chittka, L. (2017). Bee cognition. *Current Biology, 27*(19), R1049–R1053.

15. Shohat-Ophir, et al. (2012). Sexual deprivation increases ethanol intake in Drosophila. *Science, 335*(6074), 1351–1355.

16. Chittka, L., & Wilson, C. (2019). Expanding consciousness. *American Scientist, 107*, 364–369.

17. Barron, A. B., & Klein, C. (2016). What insects can tell us about the origins of consciousness. *Proceedings of the National Academy of Sciences, 113*(18), 4900–4908.

18. This improv show model of the mind is loosely based on Global Workspace Theory — first proposed by Bernard Baars. See Baars, B. J. (1997). *In the Theater of Consciousness.* Oxford University Press.

19. Langer, S. K. (1988). *Mind: An essay on human feeling (abridged edition)*. Baltimore, MD: Johns Hopkins University Press.

20. Panksepp, J. (2004). *Affective neuroscience: The foundations of human and animal emotions.* Oxford University Press.

21. Davis, K. L., & Montag, C. (2019). Selected principles of Pankseppian affective neuroscience. *Frontiers in Neuroscience, 12*, 1025.

22. See the discussion about feelings vs. emotions in *Mama's Last Hug* by Frans de Waal. De Waal, F. (2019). *Mama's last hug: Animal emotions and what they tell us about ourselves.* W. W. Norton & Company.

23. foodplot. (2011, March 8). Denver official guilty dog video. https://www.youtube.com/watch?v=B8ISzf2pryI

24. This is very loosely adapted from a discussion by the philosopher David DeGrazia: DeGrazia, D. (2009). Self-awareness in animals. In Lutz, R. W. (Ed.). *The Philosophy of Animal Minds.* Cambridge, England: Cambridge University Press, 201–217.

Notes

Chapter 6

1. Nietzsche, F. W. (1894). *Menschliches, allzumenschliches: ein Buch für freie Geister* (Vol. 1). C. G. Naumann. Translated from this passage: "Die Presse, die Maschine, die Eisenbahn, der Telegraph sind Prämissen, deren tausendjährige Konklusion noch niemand zu ziehen gewagt hat."
2. A Capable Sheriff. (nd). capabilitybrown.org/news/capable-sheriff/
3. Milesi, C., et al. (2005). A strategy for mapping and modeling the ecological effects of US lawns. *J. Turfgrass Manage, 1*(1), 83–97.
4. Ingraham, C. (2015, August 4). Lawns are a soul-crushing time-suck and most of us would be better off without them. *Washington Post.* washingtonpost.com/news/wonk/wp/2015/08/04/lawns-are-a-soul-crushing-timesuck-and-most-of-us-would-be-better-off-without-them/
5. Brown, N. P. (2011, March). When grass isn't greener. *Harvard Magazine.* harvardmagazine.com/2011/03/when-grass-isnt-greener
6. Martin, S. J., Funch, R. R., Hanson, P. R., & Yoo, E. H. (2018). A vast 4,000-year-old spatial pattern of termite mounds. *Current Biology, 28*(22), R1292–R1293.
7. Santos, J. C., et al. (2011). Caatinga: the scientific negligence experienced by a dry tropical forest. *Tropical Conservation Science, 4*(3), 276–286.
8. Kenton, W., (2021) Conspicuous consumption. Investopedia. investopedia.com/terms/c/conspicuous-consumption.asp
9. Reduce Your Outdoor Water Use. (2013). The U.S. Environmental Protection Agency. 19january2017snapshot.epa.gov/www3/watersense/docs/factsheet_outdoor_water_use_508.pdf
10. Miles, C., et al. (2005). Mapping and modeling the biogeochemical cycling of turf grasses in the United States. *Environmental Management, 36*(3):426–438. Christensen, A., Westerholm, R., & Almén, J. (2001). Measurement of regulated and unregulated exhaust emissions from a lawn mower with and without an oxidizing catalyst: A comparison of two different fuels. *Environmental Science and Technology, 35*(11), 2166–2170.
11. Data from 2011: epa.gov/sites/production/files/2015-09/documents/banks.pdf

Notes

12. Kahneman, D. (2011). *Thinking, fast and slow*. Macmillan.
13. Ariely, D. (2008, May 5). 3 main lessons of psychology. danariely .com/2008/05/05/3-main-lessons-of-psychology/
14. Johnson, E. J., & Goldstein, D. (2003). Do defaults save lives?. *Science, 302*(5649), 1338–1339. DOI: 10.1126/science.1091721
15. Ariely, D. (2017, March 10). When are our decisions made for us? NPR. npr.org/transcripts/519270280
16. Gangestad, S. W., Thornhill, R., & Garver-Apgar, C. E. (2005). Women's sexual interests across the ovulatory cycle depend on primary partner developmental instability. *Proceedings of the Royal Society B: Biological Sciences, 272*(1576), 2023–2027.
17. Eberhardt, J. L., Goff, P. A., Purdie, V. J., & Davies, P. G. (2004). Seeing Black: Race, crime, and visual processing. *Journal of Personality and Social Psychology, 87*(6), 876–893. doi.org/10.1037/ 0022-3514.87.6.876
18. Iyengar, S. S., & Lepper, M. R. (2000). When choice is demotivating: Can one desire too much of a good thing? *Journal of Personality and Social Psychology, 79*(6), 995.
19. Wasserman, E. (2020, August 4). Surviving COVID-19 may mean following a few simple rules. Here's why that's difficult for some. NBC News. nbcnews.com/think/opinion/surviving -covid-19-means-following-few-simple-rules-here-s-ncna 1235802
20. Cotton-Barratt, O., et al. (2016). Global catastrophic risks. A report of the Global Challenges Foundation/Global Priorities Project.
21. Global Risks. (n.d.). Global Challenges Foundation. globalchal lenges.org/global-risks/
22. globalzero.org/updates/scientists-and-the-bomb-the-destroyer -of-worlds/
23. Robinson, E., & Robbins, R. C. Sources, abundance, and fate of gaseous atmospheric pollutants. Final report and supplement. United States.
24. Copies of this report are available online under the name "Energy and Carbon — Managing the Risks." More info can be found in Clark, M. (2014, April 1). ExxonMobil acknowledges climate change risk to business for first time. *International Business Times.* ibtimes.com/exxon-mobil-acknowledges-climate-change-risk -business-first-time-1565836

25. Data can be found here: Ritchie, H., & Roser, M. (2020). Energy. ourworldindata.org/energy. Occasional dips in extraction rates appear to reflect oil supply and pricing fluctuations, not efforts by the industry to reduce extraction stemming from a climate change policy.
26. Global catastrophic risks 2020 (2020). A report of the Global Challenges Foundation/Global Priorities Project.
27. Thunberg, G. (2019, January 25). "Our house is on fire": Greta Thunberg, 16, urges leaders to act on climate. *The Guardian.* theguardian.com/environment/2019/jan/25/our-house-is-on-fire -greta-thunberg16-urges-leaders-to-act-on-climate
28. unfccc.int/news/full-ndc-synthesis-report-some-progress-but -still-a-big-concern
29. Milman, O., Witherspoon, A., Liu, R., & Chang, A. (2021, October 14). The climate disaster is here. *The Guardian.* theguard ian.com/environment/ng-interactive/2021/oct/14/climate -change-happening-now-stats-graphs-maps-cop26
30. Quoted in: Carrington, D. (2021, September 28) "Blah, blah, blah": Greta Thunberg lambasts leaders over climate crisis. *The Guardian.* theguardian.com/environment/2021/sep/28/blah -greta-thunberg-leaders-climate-crisis-co2-emissions
31. Rourke, A. (2019, September 2). Greta Thunberg responds to Asperger's critics: "It's a superpower." *The Guardian.* theguard ian.com/environment/2019/sep/02/greta-thunberg-responds -to-aspergers-critics-its-a-superpower
32. Thunberg, G. (2019, August 31). "When haters go after your looks and differences, it means they have nowhere left to go. And then you know you're winning! I have Aspergers and that means I'm sometimes a bit different from the norm. And — given the right circumstances- being different is a superpower." #aspiepower. Twitter. twitter.com/GretaThunberg/status/1167 916177927991296?

Chapter 7

1. Nietzsche, F. W. (1892) *Zur Genealogie der Moral.* C. G. Nau-mann. Leipzig, Germany, 38. Translated from this passage: "Alle Wissenschaften haben nunmehr der Zukunfts-Aufgabe

Notes

des Philosophen vorzuarbeiten: diese Aufgabe dahin verstanden, dass der Philosoph das Problem vom Werthe zu lösen hat, dass er die Rangordnung der Werthe zu bestimmen hat."

2. Allen, M. (1997, July 13). Reston man, 22, dies after using bungee cords to jump off trestle. *The Washington Post.* washingtonpost .com/archive/local/1997/07/13/reston-man-22-dies-after-using -bungee-cords-to-jump-off-trestle/f9a074b2-837d-4008-a0a7 -687933268f62/

3. Downer, J. (Writer) Downer, J. (Director). (2017). "Mischief" (Season 1, Episode 4) *Spy in the Wild.* BBC Worldwide

4. Roth, S., et al. (2019). Bedbugs evolved before their bat hosts and did not co-speciate with ancient humans. *Current Biology, 29*(11), 1847–1853.

5. Hentley, W. T., et al. (2017). Bed bug aggregation on dirty laundry: A mechanism for passive dispersal. *Scientific Reports, 7*(1), 11668.

6. For a history of bedbugs in North America, see: Doggett, S. L., Miller, D. M., & Lee, C. Y. (Eds.). (2018). *Advances in the biology and management of modern bed bugs.* John Wiley & Sons.

7. Longnecker, M. P., Rogan, W. J., & Lucier, G. (1997). The human health effects of DDT (dichlorodiphenyltrichloroethane) and PCBS (polychlorinated biphenyls) and an overview of organochlorines in public health. *Annual Review of Public Health, 18*(1), 211–244.

8. Pest control professionals see summer spike in bed bug calls. (n.d.). pestworld.org/news-hub/press-releases/pest-control -professionals-see-summer-spike-in-bed-bug-calls/

9. DDT no longer used in North America. (n.d.). Commission for Environmental Cooperation of North America. cec.org/island ora/en/item/1968-ddt-no-longer-used-in-north-america -en.pdf

10. DDT (Technical Fact Sheet, 2000). National Pesticide Information Centre. npic.orst.edu/factsheets/archive/ddttech.pdf

11. Cirillo, P. M., La Merrill, M. A., Krigbaum, N. Y., & Cohn, B. A. (2021). Grandmaternal perinatal serum DDT in relation to granddaughter early menarche and adult obesity: Three generations in the child health and development studies cohort. *Cancer Epidemiology and Prevention Biomarkers, 30*(8), 1430–1488.

289

Notes

12. Researchers link DDT, obesity. (2013, October 22) *Science-Daily*. Washington State University. sciencedaily.com/releases/2013/10/131022205119.htm

13. Sender, R., Fuchs, S., & Milo, R. (2016). Revised estimates for the number of human and bacteria cells in the body. *PLoS biology, 14*(8), e1002533.

14. This is a best-guess estimate: Stephen, A. M., & Cummings, J. H. (1980). The microbial contribution to human faecal mass. *Journal of Medical Microbiology, 13*(1), 45–56.

15. Planet bacteria (1998, August 26). BBC. news.bbc.co.uk/2/hi/science/nature/158203.stm

16. Brochu, C. A. (2003). Phylogenetic approaches toward crocodylian history. *Annual Review of Earth and Planetary Sciences, 31*(1), 357–397.

17. Dinets, V. (2015). Play behavior in crocodilians. *Animal Behavior and Cognition, 2*(1), 49–55.

18. Dinets, V., Brueggen, J. C., & Brueggen, J. D. (2015). Crocodilians use tools for hunting. *Ethology Ecology & Evolution, 27*(1), 74–78.

19. Huntley, J., et al. (2021). The effects of climate change on the Pleistocene rock art of Sulawesi. *Scientific Reports* 11, 9833.

20. Balcombe, J. (2006). *Pleasurable kingdom: Animals and the nature of feeling good.* St. Martin's Press.

21. Balcombe, J. (2009). Animal pleasure and its moral significance. *Applied Animal Behaviour Science, 118*(3-4), 208–216.

22. Bentham, J. (1970). *An introduction to the principles of morals and legislation* (1789). J. H. Burns & H. L. A. Hart (eds.).

23. Slobodchikoff, C. N., Paseka, A., & Verdolin, J. L. (2009). Prairie dog alarm calls encode labels about predator colors. *Animal Cognition, 12*(3), 435–439.

24. Zuberbühler, K. (2020). Syntax and compositionality in animal communication. *Philosophical Transactions of the Royal Society B, 375*(1789), 20190062.

25. Benson-Amram, S., Gilfillan, G., & McComb, K. (2018). Numerical assessment in the wild: Insights from social carnivores. *Philosophical Transactions of the Royal Society B: Biological Sciences, 373*(1740), 20160508.

26. Bisazza, A., Piffer, L., Serena, G., & Agrillo, C. (2010). Ontogeny of numerical abilities in fish. *PLoS One, 5*(11), e15516.

27. Chittka, L., & Geiger, K. (1995). Can honey bees count landmarks? *Animal Behaviour, 49*(1), 159–164.

28. UN Report: Nature's dangerous decline "unprecedented"; Species extinction rates "accelerating." (2019, May 6). United Nations. un.org/sustainabledevelopment/blog/2019/05/nature-decline -unprecedented-report/

29. Roser, M., & Ritchie, H. (2013). Hunger and undernourishment. ourworldindata.org/hunger-and-undernourishment

30. Roser, M., Ortiz-Ospina, E., & Ritchie, H. (2013). Life expectancy. ourworldindata.org/life-expectancy

31. World report 2019: Rights trends in Central African Republic. (2019). Human Rights Watch. hrw.org/world-report/2019/ country-chapters/central-african-republic

32. Weintraub, K. (2018). Steven Pinker thinks the future is looking bright. *The New York Times.* nytimes.com/2018/11/19/science/ steven-pinker-future-science.html

33. Pinker, S. (2019). Steven Pinker: what can we expect from the 2020s? *Financial Times.* ft.com/content/e448f4ae-224e-11ea-92da -f0c92e957a96

34. Nicholsen, S. W. (1997). *Untimely meditations.* Trans. R. J. Hollingdale.

Epilogue

1. Frasch, P. D. (2017). Gaps in US animal welfare law for laboratory animals: Perspectives from an animal law attorney. *ILAR Journal, 57*(3), 285–292.

2. Nietzsche, F. W. (1894). *Jenseits von Gut und Böse: Vorspiel einer Philosophie der Zukunft* (Vol. 1). Naumann. Translated from this passage: "Was aus Liebe gethan wird, geschieht immer jenseits von Gut und Böse."

Index

Index

Index

Index

Index

Index

Index

Index

gardens, 190–191

gasoline usage, 194

General Intelligence factor, 8–9

genes, 99, 100, 231–232

genocide, 116, 152
  cultural, 137–144
  of Jewish children, 143

Germany, 244

Gideons International, 228

Giles, Deborah, 92

Gladwell, Malcolm, 201

Global Catastrophic Risks Report,
  217

Global Challenges Foundation, 54,
  213–214

global extinction, 218, 220

global warming. *see* climate change

goats, 93

Goldstein, Daniel, 202

gorillas, 71

gravity, 31, 37

Gray, John, 252

Greece, ancient, 45

Green, Jody, 228

Green Bank, W. Va., 10

greenhouse gas emissions, 54, 194,
  214–216, 219, 246

Greenwood, Sally, 56–57, 63

grief, 92–93, 95

The Guardian, 86, 92, 166

guilt, 180–181

guppies, 245

Halifax, N.S., 253

Hall, Jeffrey C., 101

Hansen, James, 215–216

happiness. *see* pleasure

Harvard Business Review, 84

Harvard University, 251

hats, 30–31

Hawaii, 148

heat waves, 219

Heinrich, Bernd, 37–38

Helicobacter pylori, 48

Helsinki, Finland, 86

heuristics, 174, 200–203, 206, 207

Highclere Castle, 191

Hippocrates, 45

Hiroshima, 213

Hitler, Adolf, 14, 244

Hohlenstein-Stadel cave, 29

homeostatic sensations, 181–182

Homo erectus, 26

homophobia, 149, 152–153

Homo sapiens, 26–29, 41, 111, 113

homosexuality, 147–153

honor by suicide, 122–124

Horse & Hound magazine, 59

How Animals Grieve (King), 93, 96

Howard, Jules, 92

How We Decide (Lehrer), 202

Hrdy, Sarah Blaffer, 145, 147

Hsu, Ming, 131

human exceptionalism, 223–256
  and complexity, 232–236
  failures of, 223–232
  and future of human intelligence,
    250–253
  and pleasure, 247–250, 254–256
  and value of human intelligence,
    239–247
  and "winning," 237–239

human intelligence, 250–253

human moral sense, 133–136

human population, 48–49

humans
  causal inference of, 25–33
  death wisdom of, 111–114

Index

Index

Index

Index

Index

Index

Index

About the Author

Justin Gregg is a senior research associate with the Dolphin Communication Project and an adjunct professor at St. Francis Xavier University, where he lectures on animal behavior and cognition. Originally from Vermont, Justin studied the echolocation abilities of wild dolphins in Japan and the Bahamas. He currently lives in rural Nova Scotia where he writes about science and contemplates the inner lives of the crows that live near his home.